Napalm &
Silly Putty

ALSO BY GEORGE CARLIN

Brain Droppings

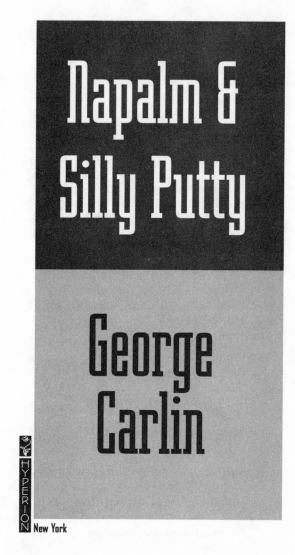

Napalm & Silly Putty

George Carlin

HYPERION New York

Book design by Richard Oriolo

LIBRARY OF CONGRESS
CATALOGING-IN-PUBLICATION DATA

Carlin, George.
  Napalm & silly putty / George Carlin.
      p.   cm.
    ISBN 0-7868-6413-3
    1. American wit and humor.   I. Title: Napalm and silly putty.   II. Title.

PN6162.C276 2001
818'.5402—dc21   00-054055

          Paperback ISBN 0-7868-8758-3

          FIRST PAPERBACK EDITION

          10 9 8 7 6 5 4 3 2 1

To sweet Sarah Jane,
the keeper of my magic.

Acknowledgments

To begin, I would like to acknowledge those of you who read *Brain Droppings*. It did better than I expected, and I want to say thanks. By the way, if you haven't read it yet, fear not. You can read this first and then rush out to the store to get *Brain Droppings*. The two are not sequential.

For those who did read the first book, you'll find this is the same sort of drivel. Good, funny, occasionally smart, but essentially drivel.

Thanks also to my boyhood friends from 123rd Street and Amsterdam Avenue who listened to my street-corner and hallway monologues when I was thirteen and gladdened my young heart by saying, "Georgie, you're fuckin' crazy!"

Most of all, thanks to my editor, Jennifer Lang, for her patience and support, and for putting these thoughts of mine in order.

Many native traditions held clowns and tricksters as essential to any contact with the sacred. People could not pray until they had laughed, because laughter opens and frees from rigid preconception. Humans had to have tricksters within the most sacred ceremonies lest they forget the sacred comes through upset, reversal, surprise. The trickster in most native traditions is essential to creation, to birth.

—*Professor Byrd Gibbens,*
Professor of English,
University of Arkansas at Little Rock.
From a letter to the author.

Those who dance are considered insane by those who can't hear the music.

—*Anon.*

If you can't dance you fuck a lot of waitresses.

—*Voltaire*

Sometimes gum looks like a penny.

—*Sally Wade*

Introduction

Hi, reader. I hope you're feeling well, and I hope your family is prospering in the new global economy. At least to the extent they deserve. For the next few hundred pages I will be your content provider.

Regarding the title of this book, *Napalm & Silly Putty*: Sometime ago I was struck by the fact that, among many other wondrous things, Man has had the imagination to invent two such distinctly different products. One, a flaming, jellied gasoline used to create fire, death, and destruction; the other, a claylike mass good for throwing, bouncing, smashing, or pressing against a comic strip so you can look at a backwards picture of Popeye. I think the title serves as a fairly good metaphor for Man's dual nature, while also providing an apt description of the kinds of thoughts that occupy me, both in this book and in my daily life: on the one hand, I kind of like it when a lot of people die, and on the other I always wonder how many unused frequent-flier miles they had.

The only difference between lilies and turds is whatever difference humans have agreed upon; and I don't always agree.

Napalm &
Silly Putty

CARS AND DRIVING: PART ONE

Ridin' or Drivin'?

You wanna go for a ride? Okay, let's go for a ride. Well, actually, *you'll* go for a ride, I'll go for a drive. The one who drives the car goes for a drive. The other person goes for a ride. Most folks aren't aware of that. Tell 'em when they're gettin' into your car. Say, "You assholes are goin' for a ride, *I'm* goin' for a drive. 'Cause I'm the one who's makin' the payments on this shit-box."

Gettin' in the Car

Now, for purposes of description, you'll have to picture my car: an old, poorly maintained, dangerous collection of faulty parts from that wonderful time before safety became such a big goddamn deal in this country. And my car is like any other small car—real hard to get into. That's important, because, after all, you gotta get into the car first. Otherwise, the way I look at it, you ain't goin' nowhere.

And let's not forget, with *any* kind of car, just opening the driver's door and getting in involves a certain amount of risk. Have you noticed that? The terrific way they designed cars so the driver's door opens right out into the middle of goddamn traffic? Jesus! About the only intelligent thing the British ever did was putting that driver's seat right over there near the curb where it belongs. Of course then they went and moved the curb to the wrong side of the street.

Park like a Man

Anyway, like I said, no small car is easy to get into, but especially if you park the way I do: illegally, two feet out from the curb, on a busy, high-speed thoroughfare right in the middle of rush hour. And that sort of car entry is even riskier if you've got a two-door, and you're tryin' to stuff a coupla shopping bags full of groceries into the backseat while everyone else is zippin' past you, close enough to smell your breath.

Holy shit! Look out!! Here comes a drunken bus driver! Quick! Abandon groceries! Stand up straight! Squeeze against the car and pull that door as close to your body as you can, taking care of course not to cut off circulation to your feet. Holy shit, that was close! Good thing you went into emergency mode. And be honest, you didn't really need them groceries, did ya? Goddamn! Look at how flat that bus made everything; imagine a flank steak with tread marks. And might that just possibly be potato juice on the ground?

Handle with Care

Now, one more thing about car entry: my car has got one of them tricky kinda door handles that're recessed a little bit into the door itself. You know the ones I mean? Where your fingers actually go in a little bit, past the surface of the car, till you grab ahold of the handle? Don't ya like them? I do. That's why they don't make 'em anymore. They found out I like 'em. That's the way it is with everything. They find out I like it, they stop makin' it.

Open and Shut Case

Anyway, back to my car. I also got me one of them doors that when you open it, it swings a-a-a-all the way open. You know the kind I mean? *A-A-A-All* the way open; perpendicular to the car. I ain't got one of them fancy doors that hangs out there halfway and stays where you want it to. With my door, we got two things, open and shut. Pick one.

And if I should be tryin' to do somethin' really tricky, like get into the car? Well, in a case like that I gotta prop the door open with a broom handle. 'Cause otherwise, sure as hell, soon as I'm halfway in, that door's gonna swing back hard as it can and sever my leg just below the knee.

"Eeeeeyyyyaaaaaaaiiiiiaaaahhhhooooooooo!"

God! That shit hurts for about a year and a half, don't it? And them huge, purple blotches? Seems like they never go away.

An Up Front Guy

Now, I wanna mention one additional problem I have when I'm gettin' into my car. Like I told ya, it's kinda old, and upkeep has been minimal, so there's another thing I gotta deal with. A long time ago, my driver's seat got pushed way up forward on the runners about as far as it goes, and apparently it ain't never comin' back.

You see, what happened was, years ago, about thirty or forty of them little pop-top beer-can rings got wedged into the seat tracks, and now they're all fused into one solid piece of metal, and that fuckin' seat ain't never gonna move again. Unless, of course, there's an atomic attack, in which case it probably ain't gonna budge more than an inch or two.

So, because of all this unintentional seat redesign, when I get into full drivin' mode, I'm pretty much hangin' out right behind the radiator. In fact, if I wanna check my speedo, I gotta look straight down into my crotch. But, hey! At least I'm in the car.

Tight Squeeze

But maybe you're not! Maybe I oughta mention one more common car reentry problem: I know that some of you fainthearted folks like to play it safe by parkin' right in the mall parking lot. And, of course when you park the car, you do so in such a manner that leaves you full access to the door. But while you're in the mall chargin' all that worthless merchandise, some asshole parks right next to you, leaves about six inches between cars, and now you can't get your door open more than three or four degrees at best.

So, in order to gain access, you gotta try to wedge yourself through a tiny little crack, while balancing six gift-wrapped packages, all the time maintaining the integrity of a lit cigarette hangin' off your lip. Besides which, your own particular lumbar spine is not the best one God ever put together, and everybody knows that even a *proper* back is not made for gettin' into a car under circumstances such as these.

And, by the way, as most men know, tryin' to squeeze into a car in that manner also creates a potential for serious ball-injury from the steering wheel. Many's the family-planning program that's gone out the window due to poor parking. Solution: Always park way down at the far end of the lot, where the homeless people live. Your back and your balls will thank you. And the walk'll do ya good.

Door #4

Anyway, at this point I think we're all in the car, so now I'll just reach over here and . . . I'll just reach over here and . . . awww, shit! Goddamn door is still wide open. Well, maybe if I lean wa-a-ay out, and stretch my arm as far as it'll go; maybe without actually getting up, I can just reach out and . . . uuuuuhhhnnggh! Fuck it! It appears, folks, that today we're gonna be driving with the door wide open. What the heck, it's a lovely day, and they say an open driver's door actually helps you a little bit on left-hand turns. Acts like a rudder, increasing the drag factor on the port side.

Idiots and Maniacs

Okay, now we're gonna be takin' our little drive in just a minute or two, but first a philosophical question: Have you ever noticed that when you're drivin', anyone goin' slower than you is an idiot? And anyone goin' faster than you is a maniac?

"Will you look at this idiot!" [points right] "Look at him! Just creepin' along!" [swings head left] "Holy shit!! Look at that maniac go!"

Why, I tell ya, folks, it's a wonder we ever get anywhere at all these days, what with all the idiots and maniacs out there. Because no one ever drives at my speed.

Actually, I don't let people drive at my speed. If I see some guy in the next lane keepin' pace with me, I slow down. I let that asshole get a little bit ahead, so I can keep an eye on him. I like to know who I'm drivin' near. In fact, quite often at a red light I'll ask for personal references. You can never be too careful.

Getting Started

Okay. Now, a few basic points about driving. One of the first things they teach you in Driver's Ed is where to put your hands on the steering wheel. They tell you put 'em at ten o'clock and two o'clock. Never mind that. I put mine at 9:45 and 2:17. Gives me an extra half hour to get where I'm goin'.

Some Things Break Easy

Now, most drivers know that some things that happen in the car can cause great embarrassment. I've never done any of these things myself, of course, but I'm sure you'll recognize a few of them. Here's a good example: you ever been driving someone else's car, and for some reason they're in the car, too? You know what I mean? Let's say they got pushed off the balcony of a crack house and broke both their ankles, and they can't drive, so you're takin' them out to buy some crack? You're drivin' their car? But *you're* used to driving *your* car. And their gear shift handle is mounted on the opposite side from where yours is, and suddenly you go to shift gears and [CRACK!] break their fuckin' turn signal off! Just break it clean off the steering column!

"Holy shit, came right off, didn't it? God damn! You'll have to get a *new* one of them! Here, throw this old one out the window! It ain't no good to ya now. Shit, that broke easy, didn't it?"

Some things break easy. Just break right off. Like radio dials. The old kind, the knob kind. Damn, those things were fragile. You'd be drivin' along just tryin' to tune in somethin' on the radio. Tryin' to find some kinda music you could actually tolerate. And you'd just keep turnin' and turnin' and turnin' that dial, until finally you got way over onto the right-hand side of the dashboard and ran clean outta radio stations, and then . . . CRACK!!!

"Holy shit, came right off, didn't it? God damn! Gotta throw that mother away! Gimme a fresh one outta that little bag, would ya? I got about fifty of those motherfuckers. Damn, they break easy!"

So you stick a new knob onto the radio and keep turnin' and turnin' and turnin', until finally you wind up past the glove compartment listenin' to some radio station located over near the right-hand mirror. Damn. Some things break easy.

It's Your Car, Have a Little Fun!

I'm a great believer in using every piece of equipment on the car. Every feature, every option, even if you don't need it. Fuck it, you paid for the car, use everything!

Use the sun visor. Even on a cloudy day. Flip it up, flip it down; flip it over to the side like the French people do. Lower the passenger's visor, even if no one is sitting there. Open the ashtray, push in the lighter; who cares if you don't smoke? Turn all the knobs, press all the buttons. Have a lot of fun. Change the mirrors all around. Press the trunk release. Pop the hood open. Put your seat in a ridiculous position. Lower all the windows. Stick out your hand. Tell the other drivers to slow down. You have power. Use hand signals. Tell them to slow down. And then tell them to stop.

"Stop! Stop!"

Then let one guy go. Only one.

"Okay, you can go. Go! Go! Go! No, not you! Just him! Okay, *now* you! Go! Go!"

You have power. Use it. Fuck it. You're makin' the car payments, have a little fun.

EAT A BOX OF COOKIES

Did you ever eat a whole box of cookies right in a row? Did you ever do that? I don't mean take them into your bedroom or something. I mean open them right up in the kitchen as soon as you get home from the store and eat 'em while you're standing there? Just stare at the toaster while you're eatin' a whole goddamn box of cookies? Did you ever do that? Isn't it great?

And did you ever notice that printed right on the cookie box it says, "Open here"? Well, what did they think I was gonna do? Move to Hong Kong to open up their fuckin' cookies? Of *course* I'm gonna open 'em here. I'm gonna eat 'em here, I'd almost *have* to open 'em here. Thank God it doesn't say, "Open somewhere else." I'd be up all night tryin' to figure out an appropriate location.

SHORT TAKES

Ah, to be a bird. To fly the skies, sing my song, and best of all occasionally peck someone's eyes out.

When he got loaded, the human cannonball knew there were not many men of his caliber.

I don't like porno movies. They piss me off. First they show a great-looking naked woman who starts playing with herself. And while I'm watching, she sort of becomes my girlfriend. And then, suddenly, in walks a guy with a big dick, and he starts fucking my girlfriend. It pisses me off.

Most people with low self-esteem have earned it.

Haven't we gone far enough with colored ribbons for different causes? Every cause has its own color. Red for AIDS, blue for child abuse, pink for breast cancer, green for the rain forest. I've got a brown one. You know what it means? "Eat shit, motherfucker!"

I enjoy young people because they're really fucked up and don't know what they're doing. I like that. I support all fucked-up people regardless of age.

In that book *Tuesdays with Morrie,* Morrie Schwartz had Lou Gehrig's disease. But what isn't generally known is that because of a mix-up at the hospital, Lou Gehrig had Hodgkin's disease, Hodgkin had Parkinson's disease, and Parkinson had Alzheimer's disease. Unfortunately, Alzheimer couldn't remember whose disease he had. He thinks it might have been Wally Pipp.

Whenever you see more than two men sitting in a parked car after dark you can be sure drugs are involved.

You know what we haven't had in quite a while? A really big fire in a crowded nightclub. What's going on?

When I die I don't want to be buried, but I don't want to be cremated either. I want to be blown up. Put me on a pile of explosives and blow me up. Or throw my body from a helicopter. That would be fun. One stipulation: wherever I land, you have to leave me there. Even if it's the mayor's lawn. Just let me lie there. But keep the dogs away.

Isn't it nice that once your parents are dead they can't come back and start fucking with you again?

The trouble with a sitcom is that every week it's the same irritating group of assholes.

People who say they don't care what people think are usually desperate to have people think they don't care what people think.

I never see any black twins. What's the deal here?

You know what would be great? To be in a coma. You're still alive, but you have no responsibilities.

"He owes me six thousand dollars."

"He's in a coma."

"Oh, okay. Never mind."

If I had my choice of how to die I would like to be sitting on the crosstown bus and suddenly burst into flames.

Have you noticed fluorescent lights seem afraid to come on? When you turn on a fluorescent light it flickers and hesitates and is sort of unsure of itself. Then after several seconds it seems to gain confidence and light up at full strength. What's that all about? Cain't these lamps receive some sort of counseling?

You know what would be fun? To fuck a grief-stricken woman.

THE CHRISTIANS ARE COMING TO GET YOU,
AND THEY ARE NOT PLEASANT PEOPLE.

I recently bought a book of free verse. For twelve dollars.

One of my favorite things to do at a party is smoke a bunch of PCP and start taking people's rectal temperatures without permission.

If the police never find it, is it still a clue?

You know an odd feeling? Sitting on the toilet eating a chocolate candy bar.

Have you ever started a path? No one seems willing to do this. We don't mind using existing paths, but we rarely start new ones. Do it today. Start a path. Even if it doesn't lead anywhere.

You can't argue with a good blow job.

True Fact: There is now an "interactive food" called SNOT—Super Nauseating Obnoxious Treat. It squirts out of a plastic dispenser that looks like a man's nose. God bless America.

I've thought it over, and I've decided pus is okay.

Every sixty seconds, thirty acres of rain forest are destroyed in order to raise beef for fast-food restaurants that sell it to people, giving them strokes and heart attacks, which raise medical costs and insurance rates, providing insurance companies with more money to invest in large corporations that branch out further into the Third World so they can destroy more rain forests.

When I was a kid, if a guy got killed in a western movie I always wondered who got his horse.

I have no sympathy for "single dads." Most of these guys got married because they wanted steady pussy. Well, steady pussy leads to steady babies, and steady babies tend to cut down the pussy. So, once the novelty wears off, the marriage disappears. Single dads. Big fuckin' deal.

AIRLINE ANNOUNCEMENTS: PART ONE

Here's something we all have in common: flying on big airplanes and listening to the announcements. And trying to pretend the language they're using is English. Doesn't always sound like it to me.

Preflight

It starts at the gate: "We'd like to begin the **boarding process.**" Extra word. "Process." Not necessary. Boarding is sufficient. "We'd like to begin the boarding." Simple. Tells the story. People add extra words when they want things to sound more important than they really are. "Boarding process" sounds important. It isn't. It's just a group of people getting on an airplane.

To begin their boarding process, the airline announces they will **preboard** certain passengers. And I wonder, How can that be? How can people board before they board? This I gotta see. But before anything interesting can happen I'm told to get on the plane. "Sir, you can get on the plane now." And I think for a moment. "*On* the plane? No, my friends, not me. I'm not getting *on* the plane; I'm getting *in* the plane! Let Evel Knievel get *on* the plane, I'll be sitting inside in one of those little chairs. It seems less windy in there."

Then they mention that it's a **nonstop flight.** Well, I must say I don't care for that sort of thing. Call me old-fashioned, but I insist that my flight stop. Preferably at an airport. Somehow those sudden cornfield stops interfere with the flow of my day. And just about at this point, they tell me the flight has been delayed because of a **change of equipment.** And deep down I'm thinking, "broken plane!"

Speaking of potential mishaps, here's a phrase that apparently the airlines simply made up: **near miss.** They say that if two planes almost collide it's a near miss. Bullshit, my friend. It's a near hit! A **collision** is a near miss.

[WHAM! CRUNCH!]

"Look, they nearly missed!"

"Yes, but not quite."

Back to the flight: As part of all the continuing folderol, I'm asked to put my **seat-back forward.** Well, unfortunately for the others in the cabin, I don't bend that way. If I could put my seat-back forward I'd be in porno movies.

There's also a mention of **carry-on luggage.** The first time I heard this term I thought they said "carrion," and that they were bringing a dead deer on board. And I wondered, "What the hell would they want with that? Don't they have those little TV dinners anymore?" And then I thought, Carry on? "Carry on!" Of course! People are going to be carrying on! It's a party! Well, I don't much care for that. Personally, I prefer a serious attitude on the plane.

Especially on the **flight deck,** which is the latest euphemism for cockpit. I can't imagine why they'd want to avoid a colorful word like "cockpit," can you? Especially with all those lovely stewardesses going in and out of it all the time.

By the way, there's a word that's changed: **stewardess.** First it was hostess, then stewardess, now it's "flight attendant." You know what I call her? "The lady on the plane." These days, sometimes it's a man on the plane. That's good. Equality. I'm all in favor of that.

The flight attendants are also sometimes referred to as **uniformed crew members.** Oh, good. Uniformed. As opposed to this guy next to me in the Grateful Dead T-shirt and the FUCK YOU hat, who's currently working on his ninth little bottle of Kahlúa.

Safety First. Mine!

As soon as they close the door to the aircraft they begin **the safety lecture**. I love the safety lecture. It's my favorite part of the flight. I listen very carefully. Especially to the part where they teach us how to use the seat belt. Imagine that: a plane full of grown humans—many of them partially educated—and someone is actually taking the time to describe the intricate workings of a belt buckle. "Place the small metal flap into the buckle." Well, at that point I raise my hand and ask for clarification.

"Over here, please, over here. Yes. Thank you very much. Did I hear you correctly? Did you say 'place the small metal flap into the buckle,' or did you say 'place the buckle over and around the small metal flap'? I'm a simple man, I do not possess an engineering degree, nor am I mechanically inclined. Sorry to have taken up so much of your time. Please continue with your wonderful safety lecture." Seat belt. High-tech shit!

The lecture continues. The next thing they advise me to do is **locate my nearest emergency exit**. Well, I do so immediately. I locate my nearest emergency exit, and I plan my escape route. You have to plan your escape route. It's not always a straight line, is it? No. Sometimes there's a really big, fat fuck sitting right in front of you.

Well, I know I'll never be able to climb over him, so I look around for women and children, midgets and dwarfs, cripples, elderly widows, paralyzed veterans, and people with broken legs. Anyone who looks like they don't move too well. The emotionally disturbed come in very handy at a time like this. It's true I may have to go out of my way to find some of these people, but I'll get out of the plane a whole lot quicker, believe you me.

My strategy is clear: I'll go around the fat fuck, step on the widow's head, push those children aside, knock down the paralyzed midget, and escape from the plane. In order, of course, to assist the other passengers who are still trapped inside the burning wreckage. After all, I can be of no help to anyone if I'm lying in the aisle, unconscious, with some big cocksucker standing on my neck. I must get out of the plane, make my way to a nearby farmhouse, have a Dr Pepper, and call the police.

The safety lecture continues: **"In the unlikely event . . ."** This is a very suspect phrase, especially coming as it does from an industry that is willing to lie about arrival and departure times. "In the unlikely event of a **sudden change in cabin pressure . . .**" roof flies off!! ". . . an oxygen mask will drop down in front of you. Place the mask over your face and **breathe normally.**" Well, no problem there. I always breathe normally when I'm in an uncontrolled, 600-mile-an-hour vertical dive. I also shit normally. Directly into my pants.

Then they tell me to **adjust my oxygen mask before helping my child with his.** Well, that's one thing I didn't need to be told. In fact, I'm probably going to be too busy screaming to help my child at all. This will be a good time for him to learn self-reliance. If he can surf the fucking Internet, he can goddamn, jolly well learn to adjust an oxygen mask. It's a fairly simple thing: just a little elastic band in the back. Not nearly as complicated as, say, a seat belt.

The safety lecture continues: "In the unlikely event of **a water landing . . .**" A water landing! Am I mistaken, or does this sound somewhat similar to "crashing into the ocean"? ". . . your seat cushion can be used as a **flotation device.**" Well, imagine that. My seat cushion! Just what I need: to float around the North Atlantic for several days, clinging to a pillow full of beer farts.

The announcements suddenly cease. We're about to take off. Time for me to drift off to sleep, so the captain can later awaken me repeatedly with the many valuable sight-seeing announcements he will be making along the way. I'm always amazed at the broad knowledge these men have of the United States. And some of them apparently have really good eyesight:

"For you folks seated on the left side of the plane, that's old Ben Hubbard's place down there. And whaddeya know, there's Ben comin' out onto his porch right now. What's he doin? By God, he's pickin' his nose. Wow! Look at that one! That is one prize booger. And look, he's throwin' it into a bush. Ain't that just like old Ben? Over on the right . . ."

Zzzzzzzz.

AIRLINE ANNOUNCEMENTS: PART TWO

Suddenly I'm awake. The flight is almost over, and somehow, along the way, the captain has become politicized. His latest offering:

"Ladies and gentlemen, we have just begun our gradual descent into the Los Angeles area, similar in many ways to the gradual descent of this once great nation from a proud paragon of God-fearing virtue to a third-rate power awash in violence, sexual excess, and personal greed . . ."

I drift off again and awaken just as the end-of-flight announcements are being made: "**The captain has turned on the Fasten Seat Belt sign.**" Here we go again. Who gives a shit who turned on the sign? What does that have to do with anything? It's on, isn't it? And by the way, isn't it about time we found out who made this man a captain? Did I sleep through some sort of armed-forces swearing-in ceremony? Captain, my ass, the man is a fucking pilot, and he should be happy with that. If those sight-seeing announcements are any mark of his intelligence, the man's lucky to be working at all.

Having endured enough nonsense from this so-called captain, I finally raise my voice: "Tell the captain, Air Marshal Carlin says he should go fuck himself!"

The next sentence I hear is filled with language that pisses me off: "Before leaving the aircraft, please check around your **immediate seating area** for any **personal belongings** you **might have brought** on board." Well, let's start with "immediate seating area." Seat! It's a goddamn seat! "For any personal belongings . . ." Well, what other kinds of belongings do they think I have? Public? Do they honestly think I brought along a fountain I stole from the park? ". . . you might have brought on board." Well, I *might* have brought my Shoshone arrowhead collection. I didn't. So I'm not going to look for it.

Then they say we'll be "**landing shortly.**" Doesn't that sound like we're going to miss the runway? "**Final approach**" is not too promising either. "Final" is not a good word to be using on an airplane. Sometimes the pilot will speak up and say, "**We'll be on the ground in fifteen minutes.**" Well, that seems a little vague. "On the ground" could mean any number of things. Most of them not very good.

By this time we're taxiing in, and the flight attendant is saying, "**Welcome to Los Angeles International Airport . . .**" Well, how can someone who is just arriving herself possibly welcome me to a place she hasn't gotten to yet? Doesn't this violate some law of physics? We've been on the ground barely four seconds, and she's comin' on like the mayor's wife. ". . . where **the local time . . .**" Well, of course it's the local time. What did they think I was expecting? The time in Norway?

"Enjoy your stay in Los Angeles or wherever your **final destination** might be." Someone should really tell these airline people that *all* destinations are final. That's what destination means. Destiny. It's final. Think of it this way: if you haven't gotten where you're going, you probably aren't there yet.

"The captain has asked . . ." More shit from the bogus captain. You know, for someone who's supposed to be flying an airplane, he's taking a mighty big interest in what I'm doing back here. ". . . that you remain seated until he has brought the aircraft to **a complete stop.**" A complete stop. Not a partial stop. No. Because during a partial stop, I partially get up, partially get my bags, and partially leave the plane.

"Please continue **to observe the No Smoking sign until well inside the terminal.**" Folks, I've tried this. Let me tell you it is physically impossible to observe the No Smoking sign, even from just outside the airplane, much less from well inside the terminal. In fact, you can't even see the *airplanes* from well inside the terminal.

Which brings us to **"terminal."** Another unfortunate word to be using in association with air travel. And they use it all over the airport, don't they? Somehow, I can't get hungry at a place called the Terminal Restaurant. Then again, if you've ever eaten there, you know the name is quite appropriate.

A BEDROCK-SOLID ALIBI

Most vitamin pills don't have names or trademarks on them; they're just plain-looking unmarked pills. And if you're traveling with a lot of vitamins, and in order to save space you've put them all in one big jar, you have no way of proving what they are. If, for instance, the police should search your suitcase, all they're going to know is that you have a big jar of unmarked pills. And should they be in the mood to break your balls, they can hold you for twenty-four hours while they "send these little things down to the lab and see what we've got here." And you wind up in jail overnight for no reason at all.

That's why I always travel with Flintstone vitamins. Not only do Flintstone vitamins contain all the vital nutrients kids need each day, they also keep grown-ups out of jail.

"Honest, Officer, they're Flintstone vitamins. Look, there's Wilma and Barney."

"By God, Ben, he's right. Look at this. It's Dino! It's a little purple Dino!"

Suddenly, you're a free man. And a healthy one, too!

RICE KRISPIES

I had an interesting morning; I got into an argument with my Rice Krispies. I distinctly heard, "Snap, crackle, fuck you!" I'm not sure which one of them said it; I was reaching for the artificial sweetener at the time and not looking directly into the bowl. But I heard it and I said, "Well, you can all just sit right there in the milk as far as I'm concerned until I find out which one of you said it." Mass punishment. The idea is to turn them against one another.

Silly me. Big punishment! That's what Rice Krispies do. Sit in the milk. That's their job. You've seen them. Delicate, beige blisters of air, floating proudly in the milk. And you can't sink them. They refuse to sink. The navy ought to use Rice Krispies in life preservers. That's where they're really needed.

And do you know how Rice Krispies manage to float for such a long time? By clinging to one another; they buddy up. They gather in little groups of eight, ten, or sometimes twelve, but if you've noticed, it's always an even number. That's because the electromagnetic polarity of the Krispies attracts them to one another. It binds them into pairs, like subatomic particles. They form little colonies, and you can't sink them, not even with a spoon. They just come bobbing up over the sides of the spoon, laughing at you and reveling in their buoyancy. Hard to sink.

That's what the fruit is for. Not for added taste; not for nutrition; it's for sinking the Rice Krispies. Believe me, a good-sized peach, hurled at the bowl full force from a stepladder, can take down eighty or ninety of the little buggers in one glorious splash.

And I have absolutely no mercy. If I'm really pissed, I'll climb up to the upstairs balcony and drop a watermelon on them. That'll teach them to sass me at breakfast.

THE MORNING NEWS

✳ London police fired warning shots over the heads of rioters today. Unfortunately, they killed six members of the royal family watching from a balcony.

✳ A Wisconsin woman claims that last month she was taken aboard a space ship where aliens cleaned her teeth, fitted her with a diaphragm, and gave her a Valium prescription good for three refills. She also claims that while aboard the ship she was introduced to Richard Simmons.

✳ A spokesman for the Vatican announced today that in Rome a statue of St. Peter has come to life and is passing along fishing tips and veal recipes.

✳ The California Humane Society has filed a criminal complaint against a man they say is keeping tropical fish in a moving blender. The man admits it is true but says he has never turned the blender above Mix. The Humane Society claims he's had it up to Whip and Puree several times.

✳ John Barrow, a Vermont man, is suing his minister for religious malpractice. He claims the minister wrongfully included him in a prayer being said to shrink the size of another man's brain tumor. Although the cancer patient has completely recovered, Barrow says his own head is now the size of a walnut.

✳ A Florida man who wrestles alligators for a living was eaten alive today when the alligator apparently did not understand the universal signal for "time-out."

* Amtrak officials have announced that as of the first of July, all passenger service will be discontinued except for a single train that will operate only in an eastbound direction.

* Chief Justice William Rehnquist had an embarrassing moment in court last week. During an oral argument, the chief justice farted quite loudly. Recovering quickly, and displaying his vaunted wit, Rehnquist said, "One more outburst like that, and I'll clear the court."

* The Loch Ness monster surfaced today, and in a clear Scottish accent asked if she had any messages.

* A Kentucky man has been arrested for making an unauthorized deposit in a sperm bank.

* The U.S. Army has announced that although it is true they performed mind-destroying drug tests on hundreds of soldiers in the 1960s, none of the victims has been promoted beyond the rank of lieutenant colonel.

* An Ohio man whose library book was fourteen years overdue has taken his own life rather than pay the huge fine. Asked how such a thing could happen, his wife said, "I don't know. We looked and looked, and simply couldn't find it."

* And finally, here's one for *The Guinness Book of World Records*. A Baltimore man recently broke a longtime mental record when a forty-four-year-long thought he was having came to an end. When asked what he had been thinking of he said he couldn't remember, but that it would probably come back to him. He added that quite possibly it had something to do with his hat.

FIVE UNEASY MOMENTS

Moment #1

Have you ever been in one of those serious social situations when you suddenly realize you have to pull the underwear out of the crack in your ass?

"Do you, Enrique, take this woman, Blanca, to be your lawful, wedded wife?"

"Huh? Hold on, Rev." [Tugging violently at his pants] "Aah! Got it! Jesus, that was in deep. Yes. Yes, I do. Excuse me, Rev, sometimes my shorts get sucked up way inside my asshole." Ain't love grand?

Moment #2

Have you ever been at a really loud party where the music is deafening, and in order to be heard you have to scream at the top of your lungs? Even if you're talking to the person right next to you? But then often, the music stops suddenly and everyone quiets down at the same time. And only your voice can be heard, ringing across the room:

"CHARLIE, I'M GONNA GET MY TESTICLES LAMI-NATED!!"

And everyone turns to look at Charlie's interesting friend.

Moment #3

Have you ever been talking to a bunch of guys, and you laugh through your nose and blow a snot on your shirt? And then you have to just keep talking and hope they'll think it's part of the design? It works all right if you're wearing a Hawaiian shirt. But otherwise, they're gonna notice.

"Hey, Ed, check it out! Dave's got a big snot on his shirt! Howie, look! Phil, c'mere! Dave just blew a big snot all over himself."

Guys are such fun.

Moment #4

Did you ever meet a guy, and as you're shaking his hand you realize he doesn't have a complete hand? It feels like something is missing? And you're standing there holding a handful of deformed, knoblike flesh?

It's unnerving, isn't it? But you can't react; you can't even look down at his hand. You have to make believe it feels great.

You can't go, "Eeeaauuu! How creepy! Where's your other fingers?"

You can't say that. It's not even an option. You have to hang in, smile big, and say, "Hey, swell hand! Gimme three! Okay! A high-three! Yo! Okay!"

Moment #5

Have you ever been talking to yourself when someone suddenly comes in the room? And you have to make believe you were singing? And you hope to God the other person really believes there's a song called "Fuck Her"?

The American Bu$ine$$man's Ten Steps to Product Development

1. *Can I cut corners in the design?*

2. *Can it be shoddily built?*

3. *Can I use cheap materials?*

4. *Will it create hazards for my workers?*

5. *Will it harm the environment?*

6. *Can I evade the safety laws?*

7. *Will children die from it?*

8. *Can I overprice it?*

9. *Can it be falsely advertised?*

10. *Will it force smaller competitors out of business?*

Excellent. Let's get busy.

THE BOVINE FECES TRILOGY

E Pluribus Bullshit

Every time you're exposed to advertising in America you're reminded that this country's most profitable business is still the manufacture, packaging, distribution, and marketing of bullshit. High-quality, grade-A, prime-cut, pure American bullshit.

And the sad part is that most people seem to believe bullshit only comes from certain predictable sources: advertising, politics, salesmen, and lawyers. Not true. Bullshit is everywhere. Bullshit is rampant. Parents are full of shit, teachers are full of shit, clergymen are full of shit, and law enforcement is full of shit. This entire country is completely full of shit—and always has been. From the Declaration of Independence to the Constitution to the "Star Spangled Banner," it's nothing more than one big, steaming pile of red-white-and-blue, all-American bullshit.

Think of how it all started: America was founded by slave owners who informed us, "All men are created equal." All "men," except Indians, niggers, and women. Remember, the founders were a small group of unelected, white, male, land-holding slave owners who also, by the way, suggested their class be the only one allowed to vote. To my mind, that is what's known as being stunningly—and embarrassingly—full of shit. And everybody bought it. All Americans bought it.

And those same Americans continue to show their ignorance with all this nonsense about wanting their politicians to be honest. What are these cretins thinking? Do they realize what they're wishing for? If honesty were suddenly introduced into American life, everything would collapse. It would destroy this country, because our system is based on an intricate and delicately balanced system of lies.

And I think that somehow, deep down, Americans understand this. That's why they elected—and reelected—Bill Clinton. Because given a choice, Americans prefer their bullshit right out front, where they can get a good, strong whiff of it. Clinton may have been full of shit, but at least he let you know it. And people like that.

In '96, Dole tried to hide his bullshit, and he lost. He kept saying, "I'm a plain and honest man." People don't believe that. What did Clinton say? He said, "Hi folks! I'm completely full of shit, and how do you like that?" And the people said, "You know what? At least he's honest. At least he's honest about being completely full of shit."

Will They Buy this Bullshit?

It's the same in the business world. Everyone knows by now all businessmen are completely full of shit; the worst kind of lowlife, criminal cocksuckers you can expect to meet. And the proof is, they don't even trust each other!

When a businessman sits down to negotiate with another businessman, the first thing he does is assume the other guy is a complete lying prick who's trying to fuck him out of his money. So he does everything *he* can to fuck the other guy a little bit faster and a little bit harder. And he does it with a big smile on his face. That big, bullshit businessman's smile.

And if you're a customer, that's when they give you the *really* big smile! The customer always gets that really big smile as the businessman carefully positions himself directly *behind* the customer, unzips his pants, and proceeds to "service" the account.

"I'm servicing this account . . .

[pelvic thrust!]

"This customer . . .

[thrust]

"needs

[thrust!]

"service!"

[thrust, thrust, thrust!]

Now you know what they mean when they say, "We specialize in customer service." Whoever first said, "Let the buyer beware" was probably bleeding from the asshole. But that's business. That's business, and business is okay.

Bullshit from the Sky

But folks, I have to tell you, in the bullshit department a businessman can't hold a candle to a clergyman. Because when it comes to bullshit. Big-time, major-league bullshit. You have to stand in awe—in awe!—of the all-time champion of false promises and exaggerated claims: religion. No contest.

Religion—easily—has the Greatest Bullshit Story Ever Told! Think about it: religion has actually convinced people—many of them adults—that there's an invisible man who lives in the sky and watches everything you do, every minute of every day. And who has a special list of ten things he does not want you to do.

And if you do *any* of these ten things, he has a special place, full of fire and smoke and burning and torture and anguish, where he will send you to remain and suffer and burn and choke and scream and cry, forever and ever, till the end of time. But he loves you!

He loves you, and he needs money! He always needs money. He's all-powerful, all-perfect, all-knowing, and all-wise, but somehow . . . he just can't handle money. Religion takes in billions of dollars, pays no taxes, and somehow always needs a little more. Now, you talk about a good bullshit story. Holy shit!

SHORT TAKES

Do you ever get that strange feeling of vuja de? Not déjà vu; vuja de. It's the distinct sense that, somehow, something that just happened has never happened before. Nothing seems familiar. And then suddenly the feeling is gone. Vuja de.

Spirituality: the last refuge of a failed human. Just another way of distracting yourself from who you really are.

I have a problem with married people who carry their babies in backpacks or frontpacks or slings, or whatever those devices are called. Those baby-carrying devices that seem designed to leave the parent's hands free to sort through merchandise. Hey, Mr. and Mrs. Natural Fibers, is it too much trouble to ask you to hold the fuckin' kid? Are you so busy picking out consumer goods and reaching for your credit card that you can't hold the baby? It's not an accessory or a small appliance. It's a baby.

Most of the time people feel okay. Probably it's because at that moment they're not actually dying.

You know what I like about the American form of government? They've worked things out so that you're never far from a 7-Eleven.

You know what you never hear about? A bunch of Jews being hit by a tornado.

Don't you hate it when people send you unsolicited pictures of their kids? What's that all about? It bothers me. I hate to keep throwing away perfectly good pictures.

When I see a guy with hair on his back I immediately relegate him to the animal kingdom.

Every six minutes there's a rape in this country, and boy, is my dick sore. I'm tellin' ya, every day, house to house, there's no letup. It's a fuckin' hassle.

I haven't eaten an ice cream sandwich in forty-seven years.

Next time you see Bing Crosby playing a priest in a movie, picture him beating his children in real life.

I've never been quarantined. But the more I look around the more I think it might not be a bad idea.

Here's some fun: Run into a bakery and ask if they can bake a cake in the shape of a penis. They're never quite sure; they always have to have a meeting.
"Well, I don't know. Wait just a moment."
While they're talking, pull out your schwanz and wave it all around.
"Good Lord, Helen! Quick! Order extra flour!"

I don't think we should be governing ourselves. What we need is a king, and every now and then if the king's not doing a good job, we kill him.

So far, this is the oldest I've been.

I think someone could make a lot of money if they set up a little stand at the Grand Canyon and sold Yo-Yos with 500-foot strings.

Road rage, air rage. Why should I be forced to divide my rage into separate categories? To me, it's just one big, all-around, everyday rage. I don't have time for fine distinctions. I'm busy screaming at people.

There's something I like about the clitoris, but I can't quite put my finger on it.

Driving is fun. Did you ever run over a guy? And then you panic? So you back up and run over him again? You ever notice the second crunch is not as loud as the first? I think it's because the guy already has tread marks on him. But there he is, lyin' right in front of your car. Might as well run over him again. What're you gonna do this time, drive around him?

When Ronald Reagan got Alzheimer's disease, how could they tell?

Sometimes they say the winds are calm. Well, if they're calm, they're not really winds, are they?

I think a good title for a travel book would be *Doorway to Norway.*

Next time they give you all that civic bullshit about voting, keep in mind that Hitler was elected in a full, free democratic election.

Would somebody please tell me what is so sacred about the Lincoln Bedroom? If it were the Ulysses S. Grant Bedroom, do you think people would've been as annoyed that Clinton rented it out to campaign donors? No. It's just the bullshit Lincoln myth that caused the uproar.

Why do they keep trotting out this Billy Graham character? He has nothing to say, and basically no one gives a fuck.

Murder investigators say that in most cases husbands kill wives, wives kill husbands, children kill parents, and parents kill children. Thank God for a little sanity in the world.

Regarding the Boy Scouts, I'm very suspicious of any organization that has a handbook.

If there really are multiple universes, what do they call the thing they're all a part of?

Where did this idea come from that if you're a celebrity, and something bad happens to you, you have to devote your life to eliminating the same problem for everyone else? Michael J. Fox, Christopher Reeve, Mary Tyler Moore; they all work on curing their own afflictions. Why doesn't a celebrity with milk leg ever do something about dandy fever? How about an actor with woolsorter's disease raising money for the victims of swimming pool granuloma? That's the trouble with Hollywood, no imagination.

Instead of warning pregnant women not to drink, I think female alcoholics ought to be told not to fuck.

YOUR CHILDREN ARE OVERRATED

Something else I'm getting tired of in this country is all this stupid bullshit I have to listen to about children. That's all you hear anymore, children: "Help the children, save the children, protect the children." You know what I say? Fuck the children! Fuck 'em! Fuck kids; they're getting entirely too much attention.

And I know what some of you are thinking: "Jesus, he's not going to attack children, is he?" Yes he is! He's going to attack children. And remember, this is Mr. Conductor talking; I know what I'm talking about.

And I also know that all you boring single dads and working moms, who think you're such fuckin' heroes, aren't gonna like this, but somebody's gotta tell you for your own good: your children are overrated and overvalued, and you've turned them into little cult objects. You have a child fetish, and it's not healthy. And don't give me all that weak shit, "Well, I love my children." Fuck you! Everybody loves their children; it doesn't make you special.

John Wayne Gacy loved his children. Yes, he did. He kept 'em all right out in the yard, near the garage. That's not what I'm talking about. What I'm talking about is this constant, mindless yammering in the media, this neurotic fixation that suggests somehow everything—*everything*—has to revolve around the lives of children. It's completely out of balance.

Let's Get Real

Listen, there are a couple of things about kids you have to remember. First of all, they're not all cute. In fact, if you look at 'em real close, most of them are rather unpleasant looking. And a lot of them don't smell too good either. The little ones in particular seem to have a kind of urine and sour-milk combination that I don't care for at all. Stay with me on this folks, the sooner you face it the better off you're gonna be.

Second premise: not all children are smart and clever. Got that? Kids are like any other group of people: a few winners, a whole lot of losers! This country is *filled* with loser kids who simply . . . aren't . . . going anywhere! And there's nothing you can do about it, folks. Nothing! You can't save 'em all. You can't do it. You gotta let 'em go; you gotta cut 'em loose; you gotta stop overprotecting them, because you're making 'em too soft. Today's kids are way too soft.

Safe *and* Sorry

For one thing, there's too much emphasis on safety and safety equipment: childproof medicine bottles, fireproof pajamas, child restraints, car seats. And helmets! Bicycle, baseball, skateboard, scooter helmets. Kids have to wear helmets now for everything but jerking off. Grown-ups have taken all the fun out of being a kid, just to save a few thousand lives. It's pathetic.

What's happened is, these baby boomers, these soft, fruity baby boomers, have raised an entire generation of soft, fruity kids who aren't even allowed to have hazardous toys, for Chrissakes! Hazardous toys, shit! Whatever happened to natural selection? Survival of the fittest? The kid who swallows too many marbles doesn't grow up to have kids of his own. Simple stuff. Nature knows best!

We're saving entirely too many lives in this country—of *all* ages! Nature should be permitted to do its job weeding out and killing off the weak and sickly and ignorant people, without interference from airbags and batting helmets. We're lowering the human gene pool! If these ideas bother you, just think of them as passive eugenics.

New Math

Here's another example of overprotection for these kids, and you've seen this one on the news. Did you ever notice that every time some guy with an AK-47 strolls into the school yard and kills three or four of these fuckin' kids and a couple of teachers, the next day the school is overrun with psychologists and psychiatrists and grief counselors and trauma therapists, trying to help the children cope?

Shit! When I was a kid, and some guy came to our school and killed three or four of us, we went right on with our arithmetic: "Thirty-five classmates minus four equals thirty-one." We were tough! I say if a kid can handle the violence at home, he oughta be able to handle the violence at school.

Out of Uniform

Another bunch of ignorant bullshit about your children: school uniforms. Bad theory! The idea that if kids wear uniforms to school, it helps keep order. Hey! Don't these schools do enough damage makin' all these children *think* alike? Now they're gonna get 'em to *look* alike, too?

And it's not even a new idea; I first saw it in old newsreels from the 1930s, but it was hard to understand, because the narration was in German! But the uniforms looked beautiful. And the children did everything they were told and never questioned authority. Gee, I wonder why someone would want to put our children in uniforms. Can't imagine.

And one more item about children: this superstitious nonsense of blaming tobacco companies for kids who smoke. Listen! Kids don't smoke because a camel in sunglasses tells them to. They smoke for the same reasons adults do, because it's an enjoyable activity that relieves anxiety and depression.

And you'd be anxious and depressed too if you had to put up with pathetic, insecure, yuppie parents who enroll you in college before you've even figured out which side of the playpen smells the worst and then fill you full of Ritalin to get you in a mood *they* approve of, and drag you all over town in search of empty, meaningless structure: Little League, Cub Scouts, swimming, soccer, karate, piano, bagpipes, watercolors, witchcraft, glass blowing, and dildo practice. It's absurd.

They even have "play dates," for Christ's sake! Playing is now done by appointment! Whatever happened to "You show me your wee-wee, and I'll show you mine"? You never hear that anymore.

But it's true. A lot of these striving, anal parents are burning their kids out on structure. I think what every child needs and ought to have every day is two hours of daydreaming. Plain old daydreaming. Turn off the Internet, the CD-ROMs, and the computer games and let them stare at a tree for a couple of hours. It's good for them. And you know something? Every now and then they actually come up with one of their own ideas. You want to know how you can help your kids? Leave them the fuck alone!

CARS AND DRIVING: PART TWO

Reverse Logic

Here's an embarrassing driving situation, the kind of thing that can haunt you for several hundred miles. One of those incidents you can't just shake off. Like the time you almost got killed by the big tractor-trailer, and had to pull off the road for about twenty minutes and listen to your heart slamming up against your rib cage? BAM! BAM! BAM! BAM! BAM! BAM! Well, this next thing is just like that, but this is one you do all by yourself.

Did you ever pull up to a red light, and go a little bit too far into the intersection? Just a few extra feet? So, you put the car in reverse and back up ju-u-u-u-st a little bit. And then you forget the car is in reverse? And so you sit there, innocently, waiting for the light to change. Looking around. Eager to get movin' again. Don't wanna keep the proctologist waiting. Da-dum, da-dum, dee-dee, da-dum.

At this point, folks, you are truly an accident waiting to happen. An insurance claim in progress. So, you sit some more, and you sit some more, and you wait, and you wait, and you wait. And you stare at the red light, and you look over at the woman on the right adjustin' her tits, and you look at the guy on the left pickin' his nose, and then finally—finally—the light changes and off you go! CRASH! CRUNCH! CRUMPLE! TINKLE! Directly backward into the grille of what was formerly a cute little red Yugo.

"Holy shit! How'd I get back here? This is where I was a coupla minutes ago!"

Apparently, you have to pay attention even at the red lights. I thought surely they were for resting. You know, drive a little, rest a little, drive a little, rest a little. Seemed that way to me. Guess not.

Oh, Brother!

Here's a little red-light story somebody told me a long time ago. This guy's drivin' along, he's got someone sittin' right next to him in the passenger seat, and he goes straight through a red light. ZOOOOM!

Passenger says, "Whaddaya doin'?"

Driver says, "Never mind! My brother drives like this."

They go a little farther, and come to another red light. ZOOM! Guy goes right through it!

"Whaddaya doin'?"

"Will you stop? I told ya, my brother drives like this."

He keeps on goin', and now he comes to a green light. He slams on the brakes.

"Whaddaya doin'?"

"Well, you never know. My brother might be comin' the other way!"

Turn, Turn, Turn

Now, a couple of things to remember when you're out in traffic. First of all, never get behind anybody weird. Y'ever get stuck behind a guy whose turn signal has been on for about eighty miles? And you're thinkin' to yourself, "Well, maybe he's just a really cautious man. I'm not gonna pass him now, he may turn at any moment."

And later you discover he was driving around the world—to the left!

Slow Dancin' in the Fast Lane

Another pain in the ass you don't want to get behind is anyone who drives real sss-l-l-l-o-o-o-ww. Boy, that's good for your arteries, isn't it? Someone really . . . really . . . sss-l-l-l-o-o-o-ww!

There are two classes of drivers in this category. The first is any four-foot woman in a Cadillac whose head you cannot see. This is certain death. At first you think, "Well, maybe it's a remote-controlled, experimental robot car. No, I can see tiny knuckles on the wheel and a small patch of blue hair." At this point I take no chances; I pull over immediately and take public transportation. I'm not about to fuck with a ghost car; let someone else flag down the Flying Dutchman, it's not my job.

Another driver you don't want to get behind is any man over seventy wearing a flannel cap with earflaps. In August. Keep your distance! Because, folks, you know how pissed you can get. Even though you think you're a mighty cool customer, you do get mighty pissed out there.

Gettin' Even

Don't you occasionally wish that instead of having headlights you had a couple of 50-caliber machine guns on the front of your car? So you could send several hundred rounds of burning lead into that slow-movin' gas guzzler up ahead? Just incinerate the motherfucker and get his ass off the road permanently?

Or don't you wish you were driving a rented car, so you could bash the asshole in the rear end, pay the deductible, and be done with the whole goddamn thing? BAM! BAM! BAM!

"Don't mind me, folks. I'm just tryin' to ease him into second gear." BAM! BAM! BAM!

God, it would do my heart good.

Or if the offender is directly behind you, wouldn't it be nice to have an electronic message board that would rise up out of the trunk of your car and let you type in any message you like? ATTENTION, ASSHOLE! YOU DRIVE LIKE OLD PEOPLE FUCK. SLOW AND SLOPPY!

You Light Up My Life

Speakin' of behind you, don't you just love it when there's one of those guys on your tail whose *brights are on*? Isn't that a treat? Some shit-stain who just had his headlights aimed and wants you to see what a wonderful job his mechanic did? You know how you handle a guy like that? Slam on your brakes and let him plow right into you. It might cost you a little money, but it sure puts them fuckin' lights out in a hurry. Let him find his way home in the dark.

Volume Control

Does this ever happen to you? You're driving through heavy downtown traffic, block to block, street to street. Busy area. People hurryin' home at five o'clock. Maybe it's winter, and it's already dark, raining a little bit. You got the window open, and you can hear the rain and the traffic noise. People honkin' at each other. Got the radio on. Got the windshield wipers going. Everything's happening at once: radio, rain, wipers, horns, traffic—lots of noise. And you're just trying to get across town to run an errand. And then, after all kinds of hassles, you get over there and park the car, turn off the key, go inside, and take care of business. And then when you come back out to the car and turn on the key, **THE GODDAMN RADIO IS THIS LOUD!!!**

And you sit there, stunned, thinking to yourself, "Could I . . . possibly . . . have been . . . listening to that?"

What's My Lane?

Here's one of those things you have to do every time you drive, especially if you're in a hurry. It happens as you approach a red light, and find several lanes of cars ahead of you. As you roll up to the pack, you have to decide which lane to get into. You have to guess which car looks like a good bet to take off quickly, so you can move out fast when the light turns green. With half a block to go you have to decide who's the really fast asshole in this group up ahead.

Forget the Volvo, she's listening to public radio, and drives the way she lives—with fear and caution. You'll also want to avoid that Toyota with the fish symbol; Christians drive as though Jesus himself was a traffic cop. And, by all means, ignore the Lexus with the heavily made-up, bejeweled pig-woman. She has the reflexes of an aging panda.

Ahhhhh! Here's the correct machine to get behind: a Camaro with four different shades of primer paint and a bumper sticker that says I DATE MY SISTER. This guy's a real risk-taker; full of crank, and on his way to an AC/DC concert. You'll be home before you know it.

Goin' Home

Now, one last reminder before I tow this trusty little shit-box of mine into the shop for its bimonthly overhaul. And this should go without saying. That's why I'm going to say it: Drinking and driving don't mix. Do your drinking early in the morning and get it out of the way. Then go driving while the visibility is still good.

HEIGH-HO, HEIGH-HO, IT'S OFF TO WORK WE GO

What wine goes with Cap'n Crunch? I have trouble selecting a wine in the morning. Sometimes I give up, smoke a bong full of Froot Loops, and just go back to bed. Try that sometime. Smoke a bong full of Froot Loops, go back to bed, and watch the midmorning movie. Call your boss and tell him you smoked some Froot Loops, you're watching a movie, and you'll be in around 2:30. That is, if you feel like it.

That's the way you handle a boss. You can't take shit from someone just because you work for him. Let him know who the real boss is. Tell him it's *your* job, and you'll do it *your* way. That's what bosses like—people with spunk. Act the same way when you go in for a job interview. Let 'em know what kind of person you are. Have a beer opener and some swizzle sticks sticking out of your breast pocket. Put a little confetti in your hair. Tell them your primary career is partying and work is kind of a sideline.

Tell the interviewer you'll need an office near the front door so you can leave in a hurry at five o'clock.

"I ain't stickin' around this fuckin' place after hours, I'll tell you that right now."

Let him know what's happening. Tell him you hope it's not one of those chicken-shit places where they dock your pay just for taking off Mondays and Fridays.

Then, if you still don't have the job, point to the picture on his desk and say, "Who's the cunt?" That'll clinch it. You'll probably have a nice long career with that firm. Once all your medical procedures have been completed.

SHORT TAKES

In the expression *topsy-turvy*, what exactly is meant by turvy?

I'd like to pass along a piece of wisdom my first-grade teacher shared with us kids. She said, "You show me a tropical fruit, and I'll show you a cocksucker from Guatemala." I'll always remember that.

I'm curious, what precisely is Zsa Zsa Gabor's job title?

If free trade can really turn all these Third World countries into thriving economies full of entrepreneurs and investors, who's gonna clean the fuckin' toilets around here?

You know what's fun? Go to a German restaurant and insist on using chopsticks.

I'm happy to say that during the 2000 Olympics I missed every single event without exception, managing even to avoid all the clips shown on newscasts. And although I sometimes watch NBC and MSNBC for other reasons, this time, whenever I ventured into those two locations it was with the remote control firmly in hand, ready to change channels instantly, in the event that depressing Olympic theme music or those repulsive five rings suddenly showed up.

If it requires a uniform it's a worthless endeavor.

True Stuff There is actually a TV commercial in Las Vegas that advertises a service called "Discount Bankruptcy."

There is now a Starbucks in my pants.

As long as you've decided to drink all day there's nothing wrong with starting early in the morning.

Odd Fact When two women with different colored hair walk together on a sidewalk, the one with the darker hair will always be positioned closest to the curb.

I hope we're not just human garbage drifting toward a big sewer. But I think so.

I like the fact that rap musicians are murdering each other. I don't have a problem with rap music, it's just that I like the idea of celebrities killing each other. Wouldn't it be great if Dan Rather snuck up on Tom Brokaw during the news and stabbed him in the head? Or imagine Julie Andrews putting rat poison in Liza Minnelli's triple vodka when she gets up to take a shit at Sardi's. Here's a great one: Richard Simmons and Louie Anderson grab Rosie O'Donnell and choke her to death. It's just fun to think about, isn't it?

Tennis tip You get a better return of serve if you let the ball bounce twice before hitting it.

People on a diet should have a salad dressing called "250 Islands."

Can anyone explain to me the need for one-hour photo finishing? You just saw the fuckin' thing! How can you possibly be nostalgic about a concept like "a little while ago"?

I tried to give up heroin, but my efforts were all in vein.

When I was a boy, on Good Friday in my parish, in order to dramatize the extent of Jesus' suffering, a group of the priests used to get together and crucify one of the children.

If the reason for climbing Mt. Everest is that it's hard to do, why does everyone go up the easy side?

By and large, language is a tool for concealing the truth.

What is all this shit about Dick Clark not looking his age? Take a closer look.

You know my favorite play in baseball? The bean ball. It's great, isn't it? It's dramatic. Especially if the guy is really hurt. Sometimes the ball hits the helmet, and you feel kind of disappointed. Even though it makes a good loud noise.

Do you ever open the dictionary right to the page you want? Doesn't that feel good?

Here's my idea for another one of those "reality-based" TV shows: "No Survivors!" One by one, a psychopathic serial killer tracks down and kills all of the "Survivor" survivors. Think of it as a public service.

As far as I'm concerned, humans have not yet come up with a belief that's worth believing.

People get all upset about torture, but when you get right down to it, it's really a pretty good way of finding out something a person doesn't want you to know.

How soon can we begin to execute these yuppie half-wits who name their golden retrievers Jake and put red bandannas around their necks? Apparently, this is viewed as amusing or ironic or some other quality yuppies value highly. It isn't amusing; it's precious, half-wit bullshit.

They say only 10 percent of the brain's function is known. Apparently, the function of the remaining 90 percent is to keep us from discovering its function.

Ethnic-wise, I'll tell you this: if I hadn't turned out to be Irish, I would've really liked to be a guinea.

You know the good part about all those executions in Texas? Fewer Texans.

I'm tired of hearing about innocent victims. It's fiction. If you live on this planet you're guilty, period, fuck you, next case, end of report. Your birth certificate is proof of guilt.

I enjoy watching reruns of *Saturday Night Live* and counting all the dead people.

AIRPORT SECURITY

I'm getting tired of all this security at the airport. There's too much of it. I'm tired of some fat chick with a double-digit IQ and a triple-digit income rootin' around inside my bag for no reason and never finding anything. Haven't found anything yet. Haven't found one bomb in one bag. And don't tell me, "Well, the terrorists know their bags are going to be searched, so now they're leaving their bombs at home." There are no bombs! The whole thing is fuckin' pointless.

And it's completely without logic. There's no logic at all. They'll take away a gun, but let you keep a knife! Well, what the fuck is that? In fact, there's a whole list of lethal objects they will allow you to take on board. Theoretically, you could take a knife, an ice pick, a hatchet, a straight razor, a pair of scissors, a chain saw, six knitting needles, and a broken whiskey bottle, and the only thing they'd say to you is, "That bag has to fit all the way under the seat in front of you."

And if you *didn't* take a weapon on board, relax. After you've been flying for about an hour, they're gonna bring you a knife and fork! They actually give you a fucking knife! It's only a table knife—but you could kill a pilot with a table knife. It might take you a couple of minutes. Especially if he's hefty. But you could get the job done. If you really wanted to kill the prick.

Shit, there are a lot of things you could use to kill a guy with. You could probably beat a guy to death with the Sunday *New York Times*. Or suppose you just had really big hands, couldn't you strangle a flight attendant? Shit, you could probably strangle two of them, one with each hand. That is, if you were lucky enough to catch 'em in that little kitchen area. Just before they break out the fuckin' peanuts. But you could get the job done. If you really cared enough.

So, why is it they allow a man with big, powerful hands to get on board an airplane? I'll tell you why. They know he's not a security risk, because he's already answered the three big questions. Question number one:

"Did you pack your bags yourself?"

"No, Carrot Top packed my bags. He and Martha Stewart and Florence Henderson came over to the house last night, fixed me a lovely lobster Newburg, gave me a full body massage with sacred oils from India, performed a four-way 'around-the-world,' and then they packed my bags. Next question."

"Have your bags been in your possession the whole time?"

"No. Usually the night before I travel—just as the moon is rising—I place my suitcases out on the street corner and leave them there, unattended, for several hours. Just for good luck. Next question."

"Has any unknown person asked you to take anything on board?"

"Well, what exactly is an 'unknown person'? Surely everyone is known to someone. In fact, just this morning, Kareem and Youssef Ali ben Gabba seemed to know each other quite well. They kept joking about which one of my suitcases was the heaviest."

And that's another thing they don't like at the airport. Jokes. You can't joke about a bomb. Well, why is it just jokes? What about a riddle? How about a limerick? How about a bomb anecdote? You know, no punch line, just a really cute story. Or, suppose you intended the remark not as a joke but as an ironic musing? Are they prepared to make that distinction? I think not! And besides, who's to say what's funny?

Airport security is a stupid idea, it's a waste of money, and it's there for only one reason: to make white people feel safe! That's all it's for. To provide a feeling, an illusion, of safety in order to placate the middle class. Because the authorities know they can't make airplanes safe; too many people have access. You'll notice the drug smugglers don't seem to have a lot of trouble getting their little packages on board, do they? No. And God bless them, too.

And by the way, an airplane flight shouldn't be completely safe. You need a little danger in your life. Take a fuckin' chance, will ya? What are you gonna do, play with your prick for another thirty years? What, are you gonna read *People* magazine and eat at Wendy's till the end of time? Take a fuckin' chance!

Besides, even if they made all of the airplanes completely safe, the terrorists would simply start bombing other places that are crowded: pornshops, crack houses, titty bars, and gang bangs. You know, entertainment venues. The odds of you being killed by a terrorist are practically zero. So I say, relax and enjoy the show.

You have to be realistic about terrorism. Certain groups of people—Muslim fundamentalists, Christian fundamentalists, Jewish fundamentalists, and just plain guys from Montana—are going to continue to make life in this country very interesting for a long, long time. That's the reality. Angry men in combat fatigues talkin' to God on a two-way radio and muttering incoherent slogans about freedom are eventually gonna provide us with a great deal of entertainment.

Especially after your stupid fuckin' economy collapses all around you, and the terrorists come out of the woodwork. And you'll have anthrax in the water supply and sarin gas in the air conditioners; there'll be chemical and biological suitcase-bombs in every city, and I say, "Relax. Enjoy the show! Take a fuckin' chance. Put a little fun in your life."

To me, terrorism is exciting. I think the very idea that you can set off a bomb in Macy's and kill several hundred people is exciting and stimulating, and I see it as a form of entertainment.

But I also know most Americans are soft, frightened, unimaginative people, who have no idea there's such a thing as dangerous fun. And they certainly don't recognize good entertainment when they see it. I have always been willing to put myself at great personal risk for the sake of entertainment. And I've always been willing to put you at great personal risk for the same reason.

As far as I'm concerned, all of this airport security—the cameras, the questions, the screenings, the searches—is just one more way of reducing your liberty and reminding you that they can fuck with you anytime they want—as long as you're willing to put up with it. Which means, of course, anytime they want. Because that's the way Americans are now. They're always willing to trade away a little of their freedom in exchange for the feeling—the illusion—of security.

What we now have is a completely neurotic population obsessed with security, safety, crime, drugs, cleanliness, hygiene, and germs! There's another thing. Fear of germs.

FEAR OF GERMS

Where did this sudden fear of germs come from in this country? Have you noticed this? The media constantly doing stories about the latest infections? Salmonella, *E. coli,* hantavirus, West Nile fever? And Americans panic easily, so now everybody's running around, scrubbing this, spraying that, overcooking their food, and repeatedly washing their hands; trying to avoid all contact with germs.

It's ridiculous, and it goes to ridiculous lengths. In prisons—and this is true—in prisons, before they give you a lethal injection, they swab your arm with alcohol. It's true! Well, they don't want you to get an infection. And you can see their point: wouldn't want some guy to go to hell *and* be sick! It would take a lot of the sport out of the whole execution.

Fear of germs. Buncha fuckin' pussies. You can't even get a decent hamburger anymore; they cook the shit out of everything, because everyone's afraid of food poisoning. Hey, where's your sense of adventure? Take a fuckin' chance! You know how many people die from food poisoning in this country every year? Nine thousand! That's all! It's a minor risk. Take a fuckin' chance. Buncha goddamn pussies!

Besides, what do you think you have an immune system for? It's for killing germs. But it needs practice. It needs germs to practice on. So if you kill all the germs around you and live a completely sterile life, then when germs do come along, you're not going to be prepared.

And never mind ordinary germs, what are you gonna do when some super-virus comes along that turns your vital organs into liquid shit? I'll tell you what you're gonna do. You're gonna get sick, you're gonna die, and you're gonna deserve it, because you're fuckin' weak, and you've got a fuckin' weak immune system.

Let me tell you a true story about immunization. When I was a little boy in New York City in the 1940s, we swam in the Hudson River. And it was filled with raw sewage. Okay? We swam in raw sewage! You know, to cool off.

At that time the big fear was polio; thousands of kids died from polio every year. But you know somethin'? In my neighborhood no one ever got polio. No one. Ever! You know why? Because we swam in raw sewage! It strengthened our immune systems. The polio never had a prayer; we were tempered in raw shit!

So, personally, I never take any special precautions against germs. I don't shy away from people who sneeze and cough, I don't wipe off the telephone, I don't cover the toilet seat, and if I drop food on the floor, I pick it up and eat it. Even if I'm at a sidewalk café. In Calcutta. The poor section. On New Year's morning during a soccer riot.

And you know something? In spite of all of that so-called risky behavior, I never get infections. I just don't get 'em, folks. I don't get colds, I don't get flu, and I don't get food poisoning. And you know why? Because I have a good, strong immune system, and it gets a lot of practice.

My immune system is equipped with the biological equivalent of fully automatic, military assault rifles with night vision and laser scopes. And we have recently acquired phosphorous grenades, cluster bombs, and anti-personnel fragmentation mines.

So, when my white blood cells are on patrol, reconnoitering my blood stream, seeking out strangers and other undesirables, if they see any—*any*—suspicious-looking germs of any kind, they don't fuck around. They whip out the weapons, wax the motherfucker, and deposit the unlucky fellow directly into my colon! Directly into my colon! There's no nonsense. There's no Miranda warning, there's none of that three-strikes-and-you're-out shit. First offense, BAM! Into the colon you go.

And speaking of my colon, I want you to know I don't automatically wash my hands every time I go to the bathroom. Can you deal with that? Sometimes I do, sometimes I don't. You know when I wash my hands? When I shit on them! That's the only time. And you know how often that happens? Tops—tops—two, three times a week. Tops! Maybe a little more frequently over the holidays. You know what I mean?

And I'll tell you something else, my well-scrubbed friends. You don't always need a shower every day. Did you know that? It's overkill! Unless you work out, or work outdoors, or for some reason come in intimate contact with huge amounts of filth and garbage every day, you don't always need a shower.

All you really need is to wash the four key areas: armpits, asshole, crotch, and teeth! Got that? The hooker's bath. Armpits, asshole, crotch, and teeth. In fact, you can save yourself a whole lot of time if you simply use the same brush on all four areas!

BUT FIRST, THIS FUCKIN' MESSAGE

Commercials use sex to sell things; why can't they use violence and bad language too? Not all families are as "functional" as the ones they show you on TV.

MOM: Eat your fuckin' corn flakes, ya cocksucker!

SON: Fuck you, Ma.

MOM: Why you little creep!
     SLAM! SMACK! POW!

DAD: Here, Son, try this. It's new from Kellogg's.

SON: Holy shit, raisins!

MOM: Hey, asshole! What're ya tryin' to do, spoil the kid?

DAD: Listen, cunt, I'm tired of your meddlin'!
     BLAM! POW! CRACK!

SON: Hey, Dad, when you get finished punchin' Mom, gimme some more of that shit with the raisins in it, will ya?

Advertising Lullabye

Quality, value, style,
service, selection, convenience,
economy, savings, performance,
experience, hospitality,
low rates, friendly service,
name brands, easy terms,
affordable prices, money-back guarantee,
free installation.

Free admission, free appraisal, free alterations,
free delivery, free estimates,
free home trial—and free parking.

No cash? No problem. No kidding!
No fuss, no muss, no risk, no obligation,
no red tape, no down payment,
no entry fee, no hidden charges,
no purchase necessary,
no one will call on you,
no payments or interest till September.

Limited time only, though,
so act now,
order today,
send no money,
offer good while supplies last,
two to a customer,
each item sold separately,
batteries not included,

mileage may vary,
all sales are final,
allow six weeks for delivery,
some items not available,
some assembly required,
some restrictions may apply.

So come on in for a free demonstration and a free consultation with our friendly, professional staff. Our experienced and knowledgeable sales representatives will help you make a selection that's just right for you and just right for your budget.

And don't forget to pick up your free gift: A classic, deluxe, custom, designer, luxury, prestige, high-quality, premium, select, gourmet pocket pencil sharpener. Yours for the asking, no purchase necessary. It's our way of saying thank you.

And if you act now, we'll include an extra, added, free, complimentary bonus gift, at no cost to you. A classic, deluxe, custom, designer, luxury, prestige, high-quality, premium, select, gourmet combination key ring, magnifying glass, and garden hose. In a genuine, imitation leather-style carrying case with authentic vinyl trim. Yours for the asking, no purchase necessary. It's our way of saying thank you.

Actually, it's our way of saying, "Bend over just a little farther, so we can stick this big advertising dick up your ass a little bit deeper [pelvic thrust!]. A little bit deeper [thrust!], a little bit deeper [thrust!], you miserable, no-good, dumb-ass, fucking consumer!"

SHORT TAKES

Here's some fun: Stand on line at the bank for a really long time. Then, when you finally get up to the window, just ask for change of a nickel. It's fun. They actually call other tellers over to look at you.

Regarding Pokémon, Beanie Babies, and such: something is really wrong when a major news story concerns how hard it is to buy a toy.

I don't know how you feel, but I'm pretty sick of church people. You know what they ought to do with churches? Tax them. If holy people are so interested in politics, government, and public policy, let them pay the price of admission like everybody else. The Catholic Church alone could wipe out the national debt if all you did was tax their real estate.

Whenever I see a large crowd of people, I wonder how many of them will eventually require autopsies.

Laptop. How can this be? A lap has no top; it has only two dimensions, length and width. It's not like a desk. A desk has a bottom, a top, and sides; you place your "desktop" on the top of your desk. A lap has only one plane; when you stand up your lap disappears. And your computer becomes a floortop.

Everything beeps now.

First there was rock 'n' roll, now there's just rock. What happened to "roll"? And what did Sears do with Roebuck? And exactly when did Montgomery leave Montgomery Ward? I have a theory. I believe that somewhere on a stage tonight a show will be performed by the Montgomery-Roebuck Roll Band.

I think there ought to be a feminine hygiene spray called "Sprunt."

Think of how strange we'd look if all the cuts, burns, scrapes, bruises, scratches, bumps, gashes, and scabs we've ever had suddenly reappeared on our bodies at the same time.

Regarding jam sessions: jazz musicians are the only workers I can think of who are willing to put in a full shift for pay and then go somewhere else and continue working for free.

When someone asks you what time it is, glance at your watch and say, "It's either six-fifteen, or Mickey has a hard-on." Guaranteed they'll ask somebody else.

What's with these super-cautious drivers who pull way over to the far end of a speed bump so their cars won't have to go over the highest point? Are they really worried that speed bumps hurt their cars?

Griddle cakes, pancakes, hotcakes, flapjacks: why are there four names for grilled batter and only one word for love?

I would like to open a restaurant, call it the Marilyn Monroe Café, and put hundreds of pictures of Jeff Goldblum on the wall.

I notice that unlike on other holidays, the police don't seem to make a big deal about drunk driving on Good Friday.

You know what I never liked? The high-five. I consider it lame white-boy shit. When a guy raises his arm to give me a high-five, you know what I do? Stab him in the arm. I'm tired of that shit. Sometimes I watch an old sports film on ESPN Classic, and I see a whole game without a single high-five. It's great.

When you think about it, 12:15 P.M. is actually 11:75 A.M.

At one time there existed a race of people whose knowledge consisted entirely of gossip.

A crazy person doesn't really lose his mind. It just becomes something more entertaining.

Instead of having truck scales on the highway, I think they ought to get one of those guys from the carnival and let him guess the weights.

An art thief is a man who takes pictures.

You know a phrase I never understood? King size. It's used to denote something larger, but most of the kings you see are short. You ever notice that? Usually a king is a short little fat guy. You never see a tall king. When's the last gangly king you can remember?

I hope the world ends during the daytime. I want to watch "film at eleven."

Everywhere you look there are families with too many vehicles. You see them on the highways in their RVs. But apparently the RVs aren't enough, because behind them they're towing motorboats, go-carts, dune buggies, dirt bikes, jet-skis, snowmobiles, parasails, hang gliders, hot-air balloons, and small, two-man, deep-sea diving bells. The only thing these people lack is lunar excursion modules. Doesn't anybody take a fuckin' walk anymore?

The older a person gets, the less they care what they wear. Old people come up with some of the strangest clothing combinations you'll ever see. I think of it as "cancer of the clothing."

We're not supposed to mention fucking in mixed company, but that's exactly where it takes place.

The other day I was thinking of how many peanuts elephants owe us. Personally, I'm down about twenty-three or twenty-four bags.

Did you ever start hittin' a guy with a big club for no reason? Just walk up to him and start beatin' him over the head with a big, heavy club? It's great, isn't it?

If it's true that our species is alone in the universe, then I'd have to say the universe aimed rather low and settled for very little.

INTERVIEW WITH JESUS

Interviewer: Ladies and Gentlemen, we're privileged to have with us a man known around the world as the Prince of Peace, Jesus Christ.

Jesus: That's me.

I: *How are you, Jesus?*

J: Fine, thanks, and let me say it's great to be back.

I: *Why, after all this time, have you come back?*

J: Mostly nostalgia.

I: *Can you tell us a little bit about the first time you were here?*

J: Well, there's not much to tell. I think everybody knows the story by now. I was born on Christmas. And actually, that always bothered me, because I only got one present. You know, if I was born a couple of months earlier I would've got two presents. But look, I'm not complaining. After all, it's only material goods.

I: *There's a story that there were three wise men.*

J: Well, there were three kings who showed up. I don't know how wise they were. They didn't *look* very wise. They said they followed a star. That don't sound wise to me.

I: *Didn't they bring gifts?*

J: Yes. Gold, frankincense, and I believe, myrrh, which I never did find out what that was. You don't happen to know what myrrh is, do you?

I: *Well, I believe it's a reddish-brown, bitter gum resin.*

J: Oh, great. Just what I need. What am I gonna do with a gum resin? I'd rather have the money, that way I could buy something I need. You know, something I wouldn't normally buy for myself.

I: *What would that be?*

J: Oh, I don't know. A bathing suit. I never had a bathing suit. Maybe a Devo hat. Possibly a bicycle. I really coulda used a bicycle. Do you realize all the walking I did? I must've crossed Canaan six, eight times. Up and down, north and south, walking and talking, doin' miracles, tellin' stories.

I: *Tell us about the miracles. How many miracles did you perform?*

J: Well, leaving out the loaves and the fishes, a total of 107 miracles.

I: *Why not the loaves and the fishes?*

J: Well, technically that one wasn't a miracle.

I: *It wasn't?*

J: No, it turns out a lot of people were putting them back. They were several days old. And besides, not all those miracles were pure miracles anyway.

I: *What do you mean? If they weren't miracles, what were they?*

J: Well, some of them were parlor tricks, optical illusions, mass hypnosis. Sometimes people were hallucinatin'. I even used acupressure. That's how I cured most of the blind people, acupressure.

I: *So not all of the New Testament is true.*

J: Naaah. Some of the gospel stuff never happened at all. It was just made up. Luke and Mark used a lot of drugs. Luke was a physician, and he had access to drugs. Matthew and John were okay, but Luke and Mark would write anything.

I: *What about raising Lazarus from the dead?*

J: First of all, he wasn't dead, he was hungover. I've told people that.

I: *But in the Bible you said he was dead.*

J: No! I said he *looked* dead. I said, "Jeez, Peter, this guy looks dead!" You see, Lazarus was a very heavy sleeper, plus the day before we had been to a wedding feast, and he had put away a lot of wine.

I: *Ahhh! Was that the wedding feast at Cana, where you changed the water into wine?*

J: I don't know. We went to an awful lot of wedding feasts in those days.

I: *But did you ever really turn water into wine?*

J: Not that I know of. One time I turned apple juice into milk, but I don't recall the water and wine.

I: *All right, speaking of water, let me ask you about another miracle. What about walking on water? Did that really happen?*

J: Oh yeah, that was one that really happened. You see, the problem was, I could do it, and the other guys couldn't. They were jealous. Peter got so mad at me he had these special shoes made, special big shoes, that if you started out walkin' real fast you could stay on top of the water for a while. Then, of course, after a few yards, badda-boom, down he goes right into the water. He sinks like a rock. That's why I called him Peter. Thou art Peter, and upon this rock I shall build my church.

I: *Well, that brings up the Apostles. What can you tell us about the Apostles?*

J: They smelled like bait, but they were a good bunch of guys. Thirteen of them we had.

I: *Thirteen? The Bible says there were only twelve.*

J: Well, that was according to Luke. I told you about Luke. Actually, we had thirteen. We had Peter, James, John, Andrew, Phillip, Bartholomew, Matthew, Thomas, James, that's a different James, Thaddeus. How many is that?

I: *That's ten.*

J: Simon, Judas, and Red.

I: *Red?*

J: Yeah, Red the Apostle.

I: *Red the Apostle doesn't appear in the Bible.*

J: Nah, Red kept pretty much to himself. He never came to any of the weddings. He was a little strange; he thought the Red Sea was named after him.

I: *And what about Judas?*

J: Don't get me started on Judas. A completely unpleasant person, okay?

I: *Well, what about the other Apostles, say for instance, Thomas, was he really a doubter?*

J: Believe me, this guy Thomas, you couldn't tell him nothin'. He was always asking me for ID. Soon as I would see him, he would go, "You got any ID?" To this day he doesn't believe I'm God.

I: *And are you God?*

J: Well, partly. I'm a member of the Trinity.

I: *Yes. In fact, you're writing a book about the Trinity.*

J: That's right, it's called *Three's a Crowd.*

I: *As I understand it, it's nothing more than a thinly veiled attack on the Holy Ghost.*

J: Listen, it's not an attack, okay? It happens I don't get along with the Holy Ghost. So I leave him alone. That's it. What he does is his business.

I: *What's the reason?*

J: Well, first of all, he's a wise guy. Every time he shows up, he appears as somethin' different. One day he's a dove, another day he's a tongue of fire. Always foolin' around. I don't bother with the guy. I don't wanna know about him, I don't wanna see him, I don't wanna talk to him.

I: *Well, let me change the subject. Is there really a place called hell?*

J: Oh yeah, there's a hell, all right. There's also a heck. It's not as severe as hell, but we've got a heck and a hell.

I: *What about purgatory?*

J: No, I don't know about no purgatory. We got heaven, hell, heck, and limbo.

I: *What is limbo like?*

J: I don't know. No one is allowed in. If anyone was in there it wouldn't be limbo, it would just be another place.

I: *Getting back to your previous visit, what can you tell us about the Last Supper?*

J: Well, first of all, if I'da known I was gonna be crucified, I woulda had a bigger meal. You never want to be crucified on an empty stomach. As it was, I had a little salad and some veal.

I: *The crucifixion must have been terrible.*

J: Oh yeah, it was awful. Unless you went through it yourself, you could never know how painful it was. And tiring. It was very, very tiring. But I think more than anything else, it was embarrassing. You know, in front of all those people, to be crucified like that. But, I guess it redeemed a lot of people. I hope so. It would be a shame to do it for no reason.

I: *Were you scared?*

J: Oh yeah. I was afraid it was gonna rain; I thought for sure I would get hit by lightning. One good thing, though, while I was up there I had a really good view; I could actually see my house. There's always a bright side.

I: *And then three days later you rose from the dead.*

J: How's that?

I: *On Easter Sunday. You rose from the dead, didn't you?*

J: Not that I know of. I think I would remember something like that. I do remember sleeping a long time after the crucifixion. Like I said, it was very tiring. I think what mighta happened was I passed out, and they *thought* I was dead. We didn't have such good medical people in those days. It was mostly volunteers.

I: *And, according to the Bible, forty days later you ascended into heaven.*

J: Pulleys! Ropes, pulleys, and a harness. I think it was Simon came up with a great harness thing that went under my toga. You couldn't see it at all. Since that day, I been in Heaven, and, all in all, I would have to say that while I was down here I had a really good time. Except for the suffering.

I: *And what do you think about Christianity today?*

J: Well, I'm a little embarrassed by it. I wish they would take my name off it. If I had the whole thing to do over, I would probably start one of those Eastern religions like Buddha. Buddha was smart. That's how come he's laughing.

I: *You wouldn't want to be a Christian?*

J: No, I wouldn't want to be a member of any group whose symbol is a man nailed onto some wood. Especially if it's me. Buddha's laughing, meanwhile I'm on the cross.

I: *I have a few more questions, do you mind?*

J: Hey, be my guest, how often do I get here?

I: *Are there really angels?*

J: Well, not as many as we used to have. Years ago we had millions of them. Today you can't get the young people to join. It got too dangerous with all the radar and heat-seeking missiles.

I: *What about guardian angels? Are there such things?*

J: Yes, we still have guardian angels, but now, with the population explosion, it's one angel for every six people. Years ago everybody had his own angel.

I: *Do you really answer prayers?*

J: No. First of all, what with sun spots and radio interference, a lot of them don't even get through. And between you and me, we just don't have the staff to handle the workload anymore. In the old days we took pride in answering every single prayer, but like I said, there were less people. And in those days people prayed for something simple, to light a fire, to catch a yak, something like that. But today you got people praying for hockey teams, for longer fingernails, to lose weight. We just can't keep up.

I: *Well, I think we're about out of time. I certainly want to thank you for visiting with us.*

J: Hey, no sweat.

I: *Do you have any words of advice?*

J: You mean like how to remove chewing gum from a suede garment? Something like that?

I: *No, I mean spiritual advice.*

J: Well, I don't know how spiritual it is, but I'd say one thing is don't give your money to the church. They should be giving their money to you.

I: *Well, thank you, Jesus, and good night.*

J: Well, good night, thanks for having me on here today. And by the way, in case anyone is interested, bell-bottoms will be coming back in the year 2015. Ciao.

I WISH I HAD MY MONEY BACK

Do you ever wonder who empties the wishing wells? That's our money. I've never received an accounting. It's just gone. Someone, apparently, is emptying the wishing wells and keeping the money. And I'm wondering whether or not that cancels out the wishes. Suppose it's a wish that takes time to come true. Like if you wish some friend of yours would develop cancer. That takes time. How can it come true if your nickel has already been rolled in a wrapper and deposited in a bank?

And when does this coin retrieval take place? I'm sure they don't do it on Sunday afternoon as some little girl is tossing in a penny, wishing for her daddy to come back from heaven. No, they probably do it at three in the morning, wearing black T-shirts and ski masks. I think this has gone far enough. I want to know what's going on. My friend is still perfectly healthy, and I'm concerned.

Punk Bands I Have Known

Tower of Swine
Room in My Shorts
Mary Krenwinkle's Revenge
Sphincter Hoedown
Basket of Fire
Trees for Lunch
Glandular Imbalance
A Fine Way to Die
Let's Pull Our Eyes Out
Sewer Transaction
Cosmic Groin Pull
Pudding Disease
A Rare Twinkie
Rubber Thoughts
Vaginal Spotting

The Note Fuckers
Puke All Night
Anal Lace
Gorilla Tits
Harmony Sucks
Warts, Waffles and Walter
Mess-Kit Germ Colony
Hideous Infant
Clots on the Move
Systematic Rejection
The Stillborn
Household Pest
Breach of the Peace
Thankless Child
Persistent Rain
Days of Doubt
Sack of Shit
Hole in My Scrotum
Ed, Formerly Don
Cocaine Snot Groove
Hilda Fucks
Waitress Sweat
Infected Mole
This Band Needs Practice

A CAT IS NOT A DOG

Most people understand that cats are completely different from dogs, and generally they like them for different reasons. One quality people like in cats is their independence; they appreciate a pet who can take care of himself. "I never have to do a thing. He cleans his room, makes his own clothing, and drives himself to work."

Unlike dogs, who are needy and dependent, and who like you merely because you know where the food is located, cats don't get all hung up on fake affection. They don't go nuts and slobber all over you when you come home, the way a dog does. They parcel out a certain limited amount of physical affection from time to time, but it probably has more to do with static electricity than anything else.

"Not Me!"

Cats have another quality I find admirable: blamelessness. When a cat makes a mistake, he doesn't accept responsibility or show embarrassment. If he does something really stupid, like jumping onto a table and landing in four separate coffee cups, somehow he passes the whole thing off as routine. Dogs aren't like that. If a dog knocks over a lamp, you can tell who did it by looking at the dog; he acts guilty and ashamed. Not the cat. When a cat breaks something, he simply moves along to the next activity.

"What's that? The lamp? Not me! Fuck that, I'm a cat! Something broken? Ask the dog."

"I Meant That!"

A cat can make any mistake appear intentional. Have you ever seen a cat race across a room and crash into a glass door? It doesn't faze him at all.

WHIZZZ! SPLAT!!

"I meant that! I actually meant that. That's exactly what I was trying to do."

Then he limps behind the couch, holding his head:

"Oh, Jesus! Fuckin' me-ooow! Goddamn fuckin' me-oooooow!"

Your cat is much too proud to let you see him suffer. But if you look behind the couch, you'll see him recuperating from a domestic mishap.

"Hi. Tried to jump from the sofa to the window. Didn't make it. Tore a ligament. Got milk?"

Rub Me Tender

Cats are very tactile; they love to rub against your leg. If you own a cat, and you have a leg, you've got a happy cat.

"Oh boy, oh boy! I'm rubbing against his leg! How I love his leg!"

If you have two legs, you've got yourself a party.

"Oh boy, oh boy, *two* legs! Now I can do the figure eight."

They love to do the figure eight: around one leg, in between, and then around the other.

"Oh boy, oh boy. I'm doing the figure eight."

He'll rub against your legs even if you're not there yet. You might be twenty feet down the hall. As soon as he sees you coming he starts walking sideways. He doesn't want to miss a shot at your legs.

"Oh boy, oh boy! Here he comes! *Soon* I'll be doing the figure eight."

His Ass Is Yours

Cats are so tactile you don't even have to do the petting. All you need is to put your hand somewhere near him, and he'll lean into you and do all the work. They love to push back.

Then there's the ass trick. Did you ever stroke a cat who's lying absolutely flat, and before you've run your hand halfway down his back, his ass is sticking way up in the air? As if you pressed an "ass button" or something?

"Isn't he a cute little . . . holy shit! How did he do that?"

Or sometimes if he's on the bed with you he'll climb onto your chest and stick his ass right in your face:

"Hey, here's my ass! Check my ass, Daddy! Get a nice, clean look at my ass!"

And then while he's showing you his ass, he starts that kneading thing with his paws; like he's playin' the piano. God, I hate that.

"Get him offa me! Jesus, I hate that! I don't even know what it is, and I hate that. It's as if he got hold of some bad drugs. What is that?"

"It's an instinctive nursing behavior, honey. He misses his mommy."

"You always say that. You said that about the mailman."

DOG MOMENTS #1

Fido Doesn't Care

Dogs have no priorities or schedules. You rarely see a dog with a wristwatch. Most things they do they will do anywhere, at any time. Except for the things you teach them *not* to do:

"Laszlo! Don't ever do that again. If you do I'll beat the shit out of you!"

They do catch on to suggestions like that.

But basically, a dog doesn't care *what* he does. He'll simply do whatever's next. He doesn't really *know* what's next, but he'll think of something.

He might even do two things in a row that don't go together. Did y'ever see a dog trotting through a room, apparently headed somewhere, and suddenly he stops and chews his back for about eight minutes? As if the whole thing were scheduled for that exact moment? And then finally, when he's finished chewing, he forgets where he was going in the first place and just sort of looks around, confused.

"Let's see, where was I goin'? Shit, I forget. Seemed important at the time. Well, I guess I'll just lie down here under this chair. Hey, it's nice under here. I must do this more often."

He doesn't know, and he doesn't care.

A Little Light Buffet

Like I say, he'll do anything at any time. He might even embarrass you when you have company.

You might have some folks over to the house; folks you don't know that well; people you're tryin' to impress. Hell, you might even be tryin' to borrow money from one of these assholes.

And all these people are sittin' around the living room, and you've put out some chips and a little dip, carrot sticks, maybe a little light buffet, and everybody is eating nicely and chatting politely, and the dog is lying there on the floor, in full view.

And suddenly, you glance over, and realize that the dog . . . is licking . . . his balls! Vigorously! Big, long, loving licks, in full view of everyone. And no one is saying a word.

Remember now, a spectacular thing is taking place: a naked, living creature is administering a modified form of autofellatio in the presence of strangers. Not only is it a spectacular act, it's difficult to do. If I could do that I'd never leave the house.

And yet it goes unremarked. And if someone does say something, it's usually innocuous.

"Look. Isn't he cute? He's taking a bath."

"No, Carla, that's not a bath. That's called licking your balls. If that's a bath, I'd have to say it's a mighty selective one. He's been on that one spot for over an hour now."

Then the dog trots over and starts to lick your face.

"No, no! No, Bruno! Down! Down, Bruno! Nice doggie!"

"Oh, don't worry about it. Don't you know they have the cleanest mouth of any animal?"

"Well, I'm not a chemist, Velma. I'm just basing my judgment on his most recent activity, which you'll recall was licking his balls."

SHORT TAKES

Here's a word you don't see anymore: foodstuffs. I wish it would make a comeback.

Suppose you took an oath by placing your *right* hand on the Bible and raising your left? Would the oath still count? Does God really give a shit? Does anyone?

Let's give credit where it's due and admit that Scotch tape was a really great idea.

Here's a fun thing to do on a Saturday afternoon. As you watch the football scores on TV, try to visualize each college's campus. Then picture yourself fucking someone on the lawn in front of the Administration Building.

You live eighty years, and at best you get about six minutes of pure magic.

America would be better off if we took all these male Citadel and VMI students and simply castrated them. What kind of pig jackoffs go to these places in the first place? I say cut off their nuts.

I think the blacks in South Africa should just go ahead and kill all the whites and be done with it. Problem solved.

Remembering exactly where you were when some famous person died is a meaningless exercise. It's an attempt by ordinary people to connect their dull lives to important events. Can't we discourage this practice?

There are eleven teams in the Big Ten.

The gray-haired douche bag, Barbara Bush, has a slogan: "Encourage your child to read every day." What she should be doing is encouraging children to *question* what they read every day.

"Rivera Live" is such a good show. If only Rivera weren't on it.

Sometimes when you're burying a guy alive, for a moment or two you start feeling sorry for him. And then it passes, and you keep on shovelling.

I have a friend who loves to run through Der Weinerschnitzel yelling, "Bon appetito!"

I think everyone should treat one another in a Christian manner. I will not however be responsible for the consequences.

I wonder if an Elvis impersonator could ever get famous enough so that someone who looked like him could become a celebrity lookalike. Is there room in this culture for an Elvis-impersonator lookalike? Probably.

One objection to cloning human beings is that there's a chance for abnormal offspring. Yeah? So? You ever take a look at some of those families in the South?

Why do they bother saying "raw sewage"? Do some people actually cook that stuff?

I think pimps should have an Employee of the Month the way other businesses do. It would be good for morale. And I'll bet blow jobs would improve, too.

You rarely run into a damsel anymore.

Whenever I hear someone referred to as a spiritual leader, I wonder why the spirit world needs leaders.

Here's more bullshit middlebrow philosophy: "That which doesn't kill me makes me stronger." I've got something a little more realistic: "That which doesn't kill me still may sever my spinal cord, crush my rib cage, cave in my skull, and leave me helpless and paralyzed, soaking in a puddle of my own waste." Put that on your T-shirt, touchy-feely, New Age asshole!

These days many politicians are demanding change. Just like homeless people.

I think highways should have a beer lane.

Live and let live, that's what I say. Anyone who can't understand that should be killed. It's a simple philosophy, but it's always worked well in our family.

Isn't it time we stopped wasting valuable land on cemeteries? Talk about an idea whose time has passed: "Let's put all the dead people in boxes and keep them in one part of town." What kind of medieval bullshit is that? I say, plow these motherfuckers up and throw them away. Or melt them down. We need that phosphorous for farming. If we're going to recycle, let's get serious.

True Stuff: Because of all the lawsuits against "good Samaritans" whose efforts end badly, fewer people are willing to stop and lend assistance at the scene of an accident. As a result, experts are wondering whether or not we need laws compelling us to help each other.

Joan Rivers turned into one of the people she used to make fun of.

I'm thinking of buying a church and changing it around; maybe selling crack and having a few whores in the pews.

Here's a little car fun. If someone is driving alongside you in the right-hand lane, act concerned and wave them toward the side of the road, yelling, "Pull over! Pull over! Pull over!" When they finally pull over, just keep going. Let 'em sit there and think it over for a while. It's certainly none of your concern. In fact, you don't want to have anything to do with a person like that.

Something I really don't like is claymation; that stop-action animation junk. Why don't they can that shit? It's fake-looking, and it detracts from the story.

DOG MOMENTS #2

Canine Standard Time

A dog doesn't understand time. Like a young child, he doesn't know the difference between eight o'clock and a week ago Tuesday. The only period of time a dog understands is forever. And that's how long he thinks everything is gonna last.

Y'ever scratch your dog behind the ears? They really love that, don't they?

"Oh boy, oh boy! Oh boy, oh boy, oh boy!! Daddy's scratchin' me behind the ears! My favorite thing. Oh boy, oh boy! This is great!"

And you're scratchin' and scratchin', and he's lovin' it, and lookin' up at you adoringly, his eyes rollin' back in his head, and then suddenly you stop. And he looks at you like you're some kind of diseased criminal pervert. He's disappointed. He thought the scratchin' was gonna last forever.

He can't help it—he just doesn't know what time it is.

Home Alone

It's especially bad when you go out and leave him alone. He thinks you're never coming back. Never. That must be what he thinks, or else why would he act the way he does when you finally get home? All hyper and excited and revved up like he just ate a pound and a half of methamphetamine:

"Oh-boy-oh-boy-oh-boy-oh-boy-oh-boy!! I thought you were never-gonnacomehome I thought you were never gonna come home I thought you-werenevergonnacomehome! I was so scared. I was so lonely. Scared and lonely. I didn't know what to do. I was all alone. I thought I would never eat again. I don't know how to prepare food. I'm a dog. I can't cook. I can't do anything. I don't even know how to operate a can opener. How do ya do that? What do you do, push down the little handle? Couldn't figure it out. Gimme some food. Gimme a kiss. Shake hands. Here's my paw. You want me to roll over? I'll do it. Just don't leave me! Don't go! Don't go! I swear, I'll never pee in the house again! I'll never pee *anywhere* again! Just don't leave me alone!"

And it doesn't matter how long you've been gone. They go into this speed-freak mode even if all you did was forget your hat and come back a few seconds later.

"Oh-boy-oh-boy-oh-boy! Ithoughtyouwerenevergonnacomehome! Et cetera, et cetera. Is that how ya say that? Et cetera? Anyway, I got hungry. Again. The minute you left. I was gonna eat the cat. I couldn't find him. Where the fuck's the cat? What did ya do, hide the cat?"

"Lester, will you stop it? Calm down! I was just here a few seconds ago!"

They really miss you. And they have no idea what time it is.

SOME LIKE IT HOT

Think for a moment about flamethrowers. The fact that we have them at all. Well, actually we don't have them, the army has them. You know, I hadn't thought of that; the army has all the flamethrowers. I'd say we're jolly well fucked if we have to go up against the army, wouldn't you?

My point is that there are even such things as flamethrowers in the first place. What it indicates to me is that at some point, some person, Phil perhaps, said to himself, "Look at all those people across the road. What I wouldn't give to set them on fire. But I'm much too far away. If only I had some device that would shoot flames on them."

Well, the whole thing might've ended right there, but Phil happened to mention it to his friend, Dwyane, one of those people who's good with tools. About a month later, Dwayne was back.

"Phil, that idea of yours? Quite a concept. Watch!"

WHOOOOOOSH! WHOOOOOOMPH! CRACKLE! BURN!

Before long, the army came around. "Hi boys. We want to buy 500,000 of those flamethrowers. We have a long list of people we'd like to set on fire. Give us 500,000 and have them camouflaged. We don't want anyone seeing them until they're fully consumed by flames."

Phil and Dwayne made lots of money and died in a fireworks accident on the 4th of July.

MAYBE THEY'LL ADOPT

Concerning news coverage at the National Zoo: Do you care if the pandas fuck? I don't. Why don't they stop telling us the pandas didn't fuck again this year? I'm not concerned. I have no emotional stake in panda-fucking. If they want to they will, if not, they'll watch *The Price Is Right*.

Probably the only reason the pandas aren't fucking on schedule is because some environmental jackoff has moved into the cage with them. Could you get a hard-on if some loser in a green T-shirt was taking your girlfriend's rectal temperature? Leave these creatures alone. And please God, save the planet from environmentalists.

THE MISCELLANEOUS AILMENTS FOUNDATION

Not every human ailment has a telethon to help raise money. This space is donated to the Miscellaneous Ailments Foundation. If you or a loved one suffer from any of the following conditions, open your heart, dig deep, and give what you can. And please, no small donations. Try to give more than you can afford.

ITCH · TWITCH · WELTS · WARTS · PIMPLES · NITS · SCABS · SCARS · SORES · BOILS · RASH · GASH · HIVES · CYSTS · CRAMPS · POLYPS · BLISTERS · BLOTCHES · BUNIONS · BEDSORES · ROPE BURNS · PAPER CUTS · COCKEYE · BLACKHEADS · WHITEHEADS · GAG EASILY · SWOLLEN GLANDS · EYESTRAIN · NAUSEA · PILES · GAS · CRABS · PEG LEG · ABSCESSED TOOTH · PENICILLIN REACTION · PALENESS · NICKS & CUTS · BRITTLE NAILS · WOOZINESS · HOMESICKNESS · FALL DOWN A LOT · SICK & TIRED · JUST DON'T FEEL GOOD · CHILLS & FEVER · FEVER & CHILLS · CHILLS WITHOUT FEVER · FEVER WITHOUT CHILLS · SMALL POX · MEDIUM POX · LARGE POX · X-LARGE POX · CHICKEN POX · TUNA POX · ROAST BEEF POX · WHOOPING COUGH · WHOOPING SNEEZE · WHOOPING GIGGLE · WHEEZING · SNEEZING · FREEZING · MUMPS · BUMPS · LUMPS · BAD EYES · BAD FEET · BAD BLOOD · BAD BREATH · BAD BACK · BAD ATTITUDE · POOR POSTURE · COWARDICE · TRENCH MOUTH · PUFFY SKIN · COMPLETE PARALYSIS · ENLARGED PORES · OUT OF BREATH · ARM HURTS · BAD JUDGMENT · DUMB LOOK · OUT OF SORTS · BRUISE EASILY · WIND KNOCKED OUT OF YOU · SEEIN' THINGS · THE BLAHS · THE HOTS · THE RUNS · THE CREEPS · THE WILLIES · THE SHITS · THE VAPORS · THE BENDS · THE HEEBIE-JEEBIES · SHOCK · TREMOR · RELAPSE

• BOTULISM • LEPROSY • GANGOSA • CANCER OF THE FIST • JUNGLE ROT • THE CREEPIN'
CRUD • THE 48-YEAR CREEPIN' JESUS • MANGE • GRUNGE • SORE TITS • JET LAG • ROOT
CANAL • FACIAL TICS • POOR BALANCE • LOCKJAW • CHARLEY HORSE • EUPHORIA • PRICKLY
HEAT • PEELING • MISCARRIAGE • CROW'S FEET • CROW'S LEGS • SLOPPY DICTION • OVERBITE
• UNDERBITE • SIDE EFFECTS • DOUBLE LIMP • SCABBY KNEE • TONE DEAFNESS • LOUD HEART
• POSTNASAL DRIP • PRENASAL DRIP • JAMMED THUMB • COMA • KNOCK KNEES • STRETCH
MARKS • FAT LIP • BLACK EYE • BUM LEG • OVERSIZE BIRTHMARK • STRAWBERRY • SPRING
FEVER • FORGETFULNESS • SQUINTING • SURGICAL BLUNDER • FACIAL HAIR • PLAGUE • AD-
HESIONS • SUNSTROKE • BAD GENES • SCRAWNINESS • CROSSED NOSTRILS • CALLUSES •
PREMATURE EJACULATION • STARVATION • SEEING STARS • NERVOUS BREAKDOWN • CORNS •
ORGAN REJECTION • SWELLING • BLOODY NOSE • CATATONIA • BAGS UNDER THE EYES •
FRECKLE LOSS • NO URINE • BIG EARS • BAD COLD • FREDDIE'S DISEASE • NO TORSO •
SUICIDE • HEN TOOTH • NATURAL CAUSES • CHRONIC PUSSY FARTS • ONDINE'S CURSE •
PULLED GROIN MUSCLE • CHAFING • COLD SORES • SPLIT LIP • ACHES & PAINS • TRICK KNEE
• TRICK NOSE • TRICK DICK • SLEEPING SICKNESS • LOBOTOMY • NIGHTMARES • PIGEON TOES
• DOUBLE CHIN • SHYNESS • WINDBURN • CHRONIC LETHARGY • HOT FLASHES • DOUBLE
VISION • CANCER OF THE JOWLS • CLUBFOOT • EXCESS EAR WAX • SUFFOCATION • REALLY
GROSS SKIN • FALLING NOSE HAIRS • INFECTED TATTOOS • GUNSHOT WOUNDS • ELASTIC
POISONING • UNPROVOKED WEEPING • DISLOCATED CROTCH • COMPLETE HAIRLESSNESS • NINE
MILE FEVER • MIGRATING BEAUTY MARK • UNDESCENDED TESTICLE • CHICKEN BREASTEDNESS •
BOTCHED CIRCUMCISION • GHOST LIMBS • INDUSTRIAL DEAFNESS • HAMMERTOE • DOUBLE
RECTUM • FALLEN WOMB • INVERTED NIPPLES • OUT-OF-CONTROL MOLES • TRANSIENT
SLURRED SPEECH • WATER ON THE PROFILE • SALINE DEPLETION • GENDER AGONY • NEGATIVE

BUOYANCY ▪ CURVATURE OF THE MIND ▪ INFECTED DIMPLE ▪ BURNED AT THE STAKE ▪ BUBONIC PLAGUE ▪ BLACK DEATH ▪ MORNING SICKNESS ▪ SUBDURAL HEMATOMA ▪ GRAND MAL SEIZURE ▪ SPASTIC BLADDER ▪ BRAIN TUMOR ▪ NIPPLE SEEP ▪ DRY TEETH ▪ SIX-FOOT NOSE HAIRS ▪ PASSED BALLS ▪ MIDNASAL DRIP ▪ CHAPPED ASS ▪ SPEAR WOUNDS ▪ TONSILLITIS ▪ CLAP ▪ CRUCIFIXION ▪ TOTAL BODY DIMPLING ▪ FEAR OF CLOTHING ▪ SINGLE NOSTRIL ▪ HORSE SERUM SENSITIVITY ▪ COKE BOTTLE IN THE ASS ▪ HEN WORKERS LUNG ▪ SEXTUPLE AMPUTEEISM ▪ HEREDITY FRUCTOSE INTOLERANCE ▪ MORTON'S FOOT ▪ HUTCHINSON'S FRECKLE ▪ ORIENTAL NIGHTMARE DEATH SYNDROME ▪ RUM FITS ▪ LIDOCAINE POISONING ▪ IRREGULAR GAIT ▪ GEN-ITAL MEASLES ▪ SPRAINED MIND ▪ ICHTHYOSIS ▪ LACK OF HUSTLE ▪ HYPERDYDROSIS ▪ FROTH-ING AT THE CROTCH ▪ ALZHEIMER'S DISEASE ▪ WET BRAIN ▪ PRESENILITY DEMENTIA ▪ LAETRILE OVERDOSE ▪ MUNCHAUSEN'S SYNDROME ▪ PAVEMENT BURN ▪ NASAL HERPES ▪ CLUSTER HEAD-ACHES ▪ HUNCHBACK ▪ VAGINAL CLOSURE ▪ CANCER OF THE BRIDGE OF THE NOSE ▪ CIR-CUMCISION BLUNDER ▪ SEVERE UNREMITTING PAIN ▪ COMPLETE NERVOUS COLLAPSE ▪ SIXTY-YEAR COMA ▪ RIGOR MORTIS ▪ DECAPITATION ▪ SWIMMER'S ITCH ▪ BEEF TAPEWORM ▪ SHORT-LIMBED DWARFISM ▪ TICK-BORNE RICKETS ▪ KOPLIK'S SPOTS ▪ IMPETIGO ▪ GAS GAN-GRENE ▪ TRANSVERSE MYELITIS ▪ MALNUTRITION ▪ IRRITABILITY ▪ NONPRODUCTIVE COUGH ▪ SIMPLE MALAISE ▪ EPIDEMIC KERATOCONJUNCTIVITIS ▪ FURIOUS RABIES ▪ BLACK VOMIT ▪ DANDY FEVER ▪ EUROPEAN TYPHUS ▪ BRILL-ZINSSER DISEASE ▪ CAT SCRATCH DISEASE ▪ STITCH ABSCESSES ▪ STRAWBERRY TONGUE ▪ PASTIA'S LINES ▪ AFRICAN SLEEPING SICKNESS ▪ WOOL-SORTER'S DISEASE ▪ CAULIFLOWER EAR ▪ ZUCCHINI NOSE ▪ PARACOCCIDIO IDOMYCOSIS ▪ DES-ERT RHEUMATISM ▪ LUMPY JAW ▪ MADURA FOOT ▪ HOOKWORM ▪ ORIENTAL SORE ▪ ALEPPO BOIL ▪ FOREST YAWS ▪ SWIMMING POOL GRANULOMA ▪ CARDIAC DEATH ▪ WHIPWORM INFEC-TION ▪ GEOPHAGIA ▪ RIVER BLINDNESS ▪ TOTAL COLLAPSE ▪ JEWELRY RASH ▪ TERMINAL

BROWSING · MAIDENLY HYSTERICS · MARROW FAILURE · PICA · RIBOFLAVIN DEFICIENCY · MEDITERRANEAN ANEMIA · AIR EMBOLISM · VASCULAR FRAGILITY · DRUG-INDUCED PLATELET DEFECTS · FELTY'S SYNDROME · BOWEL INFARCTION · TETRALOGY OF FALLOT · BUNDLE BRANCH BLOCK · SUDDEN MEGACOLON · RAYNAUD'S PHENOMENON · YOUNG ORIENTAL FEMALE DISEASE · INTESTINAL APOPLEXY · OCCLUSION AT THE BIFURCATION · MILK LEG · HOMAN'S SIGN · CONSTANT SCREAMING · TOTAL BODY HEMORRHAGING · MISSING LUNGS · EXTRA STOMACH · LARVAE IN THE STOOL · BEBOP LEGS · FOREHEAD TRANSPLANT · TUMOR ON THE BUNS · HUGE SPLEEN · CHRONIC FALLING · CYSTS ON THE WRISTS · SUDDEN TOTAL WEIGHT LOSS ·

Give now. Somewhere, someone feels crappy. You can help.

GOT ANY MORE LEAVES IN THAT STALL?

Recently I came across a statistic published by the Population Reference Bureau in Washington. It stated that as of 1995 the number of people who had lived on earth was 105,472,380,169. The figure was based on the assumption that "the first two people" had emerged in 50,000 B.C. So I did a little arithmetic of my own, and I've concluded that as of 1995 there had been over 987 trillion bowel movements. I was very conservative: I assumed a mere thirty-year life span and only six bowel movements per week. Still, it means that at this point there have been almost 1 quadrillion human bowel movements and most of them occurred before people had anything to read. These are the kinds of thoughts that kept me from moving quickly up the corporate ladder.

DEATH ROW

The story is that if you're condemned to death they have to give you one last meal of your choice. What is that all about? A group of people plans to kill you, so they want you to eat something you like? Is it a joke? Do they think the food part will take your mind off the dying part? Or do they just prefer to kill you when you're coming off a peak experience and full of positive energy?

I'm not sure what kind of sick game is going on, but what the hell, you might as well play along. Have a little fun; order a Happy Meal. Tell 'em you want to go to Hooter's and eat on the patio.

Inform them you've converted to a religion that embraces canni- balism, and you'd like to eat a baby. With a small salad. I just think there's great potential here for fun and mischief. In fact, I'm thinking that if you worked it just right you might even squeeze a little extra time out of them. Time to file a couple of hundred more frivolous appeals.

Because, as I understand it, they have to give you any meal you ask for. Not including elephant, of course. You can't expect them to start on a whole new elephant for just one meal. But short of that, they have to give you pretty much what you want. It's part of the humanity involved: "Let's kill this fuck, but let's be civil."

So I say have a little fun; buy some time. When they ask what you want, tell them you can't decide. That's all there is to it. You can't decide.

"Gee, I don't know. I'm not sure if I want steak or lobster. I mean, I really love them both. I haven't had lobster in quite a while, but on the other hand, I really love chicken. It's my good luck food. And they're both rich in protein. I just can't figure it out."

What can they do? Can they kill you under those circumstances? Can they go ahead and kill you if you honestly don't know what you want for dinner? Tell them you're willing to take a lie detector test and truth serum, but you honestly can't decide. Can they kill you? Can they drag you down the last mile screaming, "Surf? Turf? I'm on the horns of a dilemma!" I think they'd have to give you a little more time.

Imagine if you kept it up for six months. Think of the headlines.

CONDEMNED MAN STILL ALIVE, CAN'T DECIDE. LEANS TOWARD LOBSTER.

Three years go by. Five. Seven. And then, finally, one morning you wake up, and it's clear as a bell:

"All right, I've decided. And I don't know why I didn't think of this long ago. I'm going to have the lamb chops."

"All right, lamb chops it is. And how did you want them cooked?"

"Geez, I hadn't thought of that. Lemme see. How do I want them cooked? Listen, guys, can I get back to you?"

HUNGRY MAN EXECUTED. DRAGGED DOWN LAST MILE SCREAMING "MEDIUM!"

CURRENT EVENTS

Here's a great idea. I think Texas should save up 500 condemned people and execute them all at once, in electric chairs. Five hundred electric chairs in a big gymnasium. Wouldn't that be fun? I realize Texas prefers lethal injection, but maybe they could make an exception just this once. Or how about executing people five at a time on electric couches. That would be interesting. Put a coffee table in front of them with magazines and some chips and dip. It would be fun. Here's another good idea. If a married couple kills their kid, they should be executed in an electric love seat. Force them to hug as you pull the switch.

THE UNKINDEST CUT

I don't know about you, but I think O. J. got screwed. Double jeopardy is just plain wrong. Civil trial, my ass! It's not fair. O. J. beat the system and he should be allowed to enjoy it. Geraldo and Charles Grodin don't like O. J. Simpson. Geraldo and Charles Grodin deal in certitude. Guys like that almost always impress me.

I'm really glad O. J. beat the rap. Personally, I'd like to see him on TV again, doin' commercials. There must be something he could do. Roach Motel. "They checks in, but they don't checks out." It would be fun. We need more fun. People get upset with all the wrong things.

Like these guys Jeffrey Dahmer and Timothy McVeigh. Right away everybody wants to kill them. Let me tell you, you don't kill guys like that. That's exactly what they want. You know what you do? You let them off with a warning. Just like a speeding ticket. Sometimes all a guy like that needs is a good talking-to. You sit him down, and you say, "Listen. Jeff. Nobody thinks you're funny. Okay? No one is amused. So calm down and knock off the shit. Stop trying to draw attention to yourself. You eat one more person, and you're in big trouble."

A lot of these guys never hear that sort of thing. I think it would make them think twice before they cooked another person's head and ate it. Don't you?

Now, as to Timothy McVeigh, you've got a slightly different situation. After all, the guy's a veteran, so you have to show him a little consideration. And don't forget, it's his first offense. So I say let him off with a warning. Throw a good scare into him: "Tim, one more trick like that, and it's gonna mean a hefty fine."

SMILE!

Camcorders are a good example of technology gone berserk. Everywhere you go now, you see some goofy fuck with a camcorder. Everyone's taping everything. Doesn't anybody stop and look at things anymore? Take them in? Maybe even . . . remember them? Is that such a strange idea? Does experience really have to be documented, brought home and saved on a shelf? And do people really watch this shit? Are their lives so bankrupt they sit at home watching things they already did?

These guys are so intense. And by the way, it's always guys. They won't let women touch the cameras; it's a highly technical skill. Look through a hole, push on a button. Big fuckin' skill. And they all think they're Federico Fellini. Did you ever see them at the soccer games? With the low angles and all the zooms and pans? And it's the same three ugly children in every shot. Same kids. Believe me, all the George Lucas magic in Hollywood is not going to change the unfortunate genetic configurations on the faces of these children. Do the world a favor, keep these unfortunate youngsters indoors, out of public view.

THE NOONTIME NEWS

* In Rome today, Pope John Paul removed his little hat and revealed he has a small map of Tombstone, Arizona, tattooed on his head.

* Out at the lake in City Park, police have arrested a one-armed man who was bothering the other boaters by continuously rowing in a circle.

* Authorities say a severely disturbed geography teacher has shot and killed six people who did not know the capital of Scotland. He is still at large and they remind everyone the capital of Scotland is Edinburgh.

* A man at a tool and die company died today when he was hit with a tool.

* A Detroit couple is suing Campbell's soups, claiming a bowl of alphabet soup spelled out an obscene message to their children. They state that at first the little letters floated around in a circle, and then they formed the words *suck my noodle*.

* Millionaire clothing executive Dacron Polyester died in his sleep yesterday. It was not a peaceful death, however, as he dozed off while hang-gliding.

* A large dog exploded on a downtown street corner this morning. No one was killed; however, several people were overcome by fur. Police estimate that more than 600 fleas also lost their lives in the blast.

* A woman in Montana was severely injured yesterday when she attempted to force-breast-feed a wolverine.

* A man wearing a Have a Nice Day button was killed yesterday by a man who works at night.

* The Centers for Disease Control has determined that the common cold is caused by a tall man who carries around a bag of germs.

* Twenty-six people were killed this morning when two funeral processions collided. Police say the list of fatalities does not include the two people who were already dead.

* The Mafia has killed an information clerk because he knew too much. His replacement, appointed today, says he has no further information.

* In San Francisco, a baby has been born wearing sunglasses and holding a small can of peas.

* A Milwaukee man has been arrested for the illegal use of food stamps. He was taken into custody while attempting to mail a bowl of chili to his sister.

* The Bureau of Indian Affairs has announced they have located another Mohican. Accordingly, all the books are being recalled and will be changed to read: *The Next to the Last of the Mohicans.*

* And finally, here's a Halloween prank that backfired. It seems that little thirteen-year-old Danny Obolagotz thought it would be great fun to soap the windows of all the cars on his street. He had soaped seven of them and was starting to soap the eighth, not knowing that the owner of the car, Earl Fletcher, was seated inside. Fletcher shot Danny in the head four times.

THE PLANET IS FINE, THE PEOPLE ARE FUCKED

At some point, during every stage show I do, I take a sip of water and ask the audience, "How's the water here?" I haven't gotten a positive response yet. Not one. Last year I was in 100 different cities. Not one audience was able to give me a positive answer. Nobody trusts their water supply. Nobody.

And that amuses me. Because it means the system is beginning to collapse, beginning to break down. I enjoy chaos and disorder. Not just because they help me professionally; they're also my hobby. I'm an entropy buff.

In high school, when I first heard of entropy, I was attracted to it immediately. They said that in nature all systems are breaking down, and I thought, What a wonderful thing; perhaps I can make some small contribution to this process, myself. And, of course, it's not just true of nature, it's true of society as well. If you look carefully, you can see that the social structure is just beginning to break down, just beginning to come apart at the seams.

The News Turns *Me* On

What I like about that is that it makes the news on television more exciting. I watch the news for only one thing: entertainment. That's all I want. You know my favorite thing on television? Bad news. Accidents, disasters, catastrophes, explosions, fires. I wanna see shit being destroyed and bodies flyin' around.

I'm not interested in the budget, I don't care about tax negotiations, I don't wanna know what country the pope is in. But show me a burning hospital with people on crutches jumpin' off the roof, and I'm a happy guy. I wanna see a paint factory blowin' up, an oil refinery explode, and a tornado hit a church on Sunday. I wanna be told there's a guy runnin' through the Kmart shooting at customers with an automatic weapon. I wanna see thousands of people in the street killing policemen; hear about a nuclear meltdown in a big city; find out the stock market dropped 4,000 points in one day. I wanna see people under pressure!

Sirens, flames, smoke, bodies, graves being filled, parents weeping. My kinda TV! Exciting shit! I just want some entertainment! That's the kind of guy I am. You know what I like most? Big chunks of steel, concrete and fiery wood falling out of the sky, and people running around trying to get out of the way. Exciting shit!

Fuck Pakistan!

At least I admit it. Most people won't admit those feelings. Most people see somethin' like that, they say, "Ohhhh, isn't that awful?" Bullshit! Lyin' asshole! You love it and you know it. Explosions are fun. And the closer the explosion is to your house, the more fun it is. Have you ever noticed that?

Sometimes an announcer comes on television and says, "Six thousand people were killed in an explosion today." You say, "Where, where?" He says, "In Pakistan." You say, "Aww, fuck Pakistan. Too far away to be fun." But if he says it happened in your hometown, you say, "Whooa, hot shit, Dave! C'mon! Let's go down and look at the bodies!"

I love bad news. Doesn't bother me. The more bad news there is, the faster this system collapses. I'm glad the water sucks. You know what I do about it? I drink it! I fuckin' drink it!

This Is One Bad Species

You see, I'm not one of those people who worries about everything. Do you have people around you like that? The country's full of 'em now. People walkin' around all day, worried about everything. Worried about the air, the water, the soil, pesticides, food additives, carcinogens, radon, asbestos. Worried about saving endangered species.

Lemme tell you about endangered species. Saving endangered species is just one more arrogant human attempt to control nature. That's what got us in trouble in the first place. Interfering with nature. Meddling. Doesn't anybody understand that?

And as far as endangered species are concerned, it's a phony issue. Over 90 percent of all the species that ever lived on this planet are gone. They're extinct. We didn't kill them; they just disappeared. That's what species do: they appear, and they disappear. It's nature's way. Irrespective of our behavior, species vanish at the rate of twenty-five a day. Let them go gracefully. Stop interfering. Leave nature alone. Haven't we done enough damage?

We're so self-important. So arrogant. Everybody's going to save something now. Save the trees, save the bees, save the whales, save the snails. And the supreme arrogance? Save the planet! Are these people kidding? Save the planet? We don't even know how to take care of ourselves; we haven't learned how to care for one another. We're gonna save the fuckin' planet?

Greens Eat Shit

I'm gettin' tired of that shit. I'm tired of fuckin' Earth Day. I'm tired of these self-righteous environmentalist, white, bourgeois liberals who think the only thing wrong with this country is that there aren't enough bike paths. Tryin' to make the world safe for their repulsive Volvos.

Besides, environmentalists don't give a shit about the planet anyway. Not really. Not in the abstract. You know what they're interested in? A clean place to live. Their own habitat. That's all. They're worried that sometime in the future they might personally be inconvenienced. Narrow, unenlightened self-interest doesn't impress me.

And, by the way, there's nothing wrong with the planet in the first place. The planet is fine. The people are fucked! Compared with the people, the planet is doin' great. It's been here over four billion years. Did you ever think about that? The planet has been here four and a half billion years. And we've been here for what? A hundred thousand? And we've only been engaged in heavy industry for a little over two hundred years. Two hundred versus 4.5 billion! And we have the nerve, the conceit to think that somehow we're a threat? That somehow we're going to put this beautiful little blue-green ball in jeopardy?

Believe me, this planet has put up with much worse than us. It's been through earthquakes, volcanoes, plate tectonics, solar flares, sunspots, magnetic storms, pole reversals, planetary floods, worldwide fires, tidal waves, wind and water erosion, cosmic rays, ice ages, and hundreds of thousands of years of bombardment by comets, asteroids, and meteors. And people think a few plastic bags and aluminum cans are going to make a difference?

See Ya!

The planet isn't goin' anywhere, folks. We are! We're goin' away. Pack your shit, we're goin' away. And we won't leave much of a trace. Thank God for that. Nothing left. Maybe a little Styrofoam. The planet will be here, and we'll be gone. Another failed mutation; another closed-end biological mistake.

The planet will shake us off like a bad case of fleas. And it will heal itself, because that's what the planet does; it's a self-correcting system. The air and water and earth will recover and be renewed. And if plastic is really not degradable, well, most likely the planet will incorporate it into a new paradigm: The Earth Plus Plastic. Earth doesn't share our prejudice against plastic. Plastic came out of the earth. She probably sees it as one of her many children.

In fact, it could be the reason the earth allowed us to be spawned in the first place; it wanted plastic and didn't know how to make it. It needed us. That could be the answer to our age-old question: "Why are we here?" "Plastic, assholes!"

"I Just Can't Shake This Cold"

And so, our job is done. The plastic is here, we can now be phased out. And I think that's already begun, don't you? I mean, to be fair, the planet probably sees us as a mild threat, something to be dealt with. And I'm sure it can defend itself in the manner of a large organism; the way a beehive or an ant colony would muster a defense. I'm sure the planet will think of something. What would you be thinking if you were the planet, trying to defend yourself against this pesky, troublesome species?

"Let's see, what might I try? Hmmm! Viruses might be good; these humans seem vulnerable. And viruses are tricky, always mutating and developing new strains when new medicines or vaccines are introduced. And perhaps the first virus I try could be one that compromises their immune systems. A human immunodeficiency virus that makes them vulnerable to other infections that come along. And perhaps this virus could be spread sexually, making them reluctant to engage in the act of reproduction, further reducing their numbers."

Well, I guess it's a poetic notion, but it's a start. And I can dream, can't I?

No, folks, I don't worry about the little things. Bees, trees, whales, snails. I don't worry about them. I think we're part of a much greater wisdom. Greater than we will ever understand. A higher order. Call it what you like. I call it The Big Electron. The Big Electron. It doesn't punish, it doesn't reward, and it doesn't judge. It just is. And so are we. For a little while. See ya.

SHORT TAKES

You know what we need? Black Jell-O.

I don't understand why prostitution is illegal. Selling is legal, fucking is legal. So, why isn't it legal to sell fucking? Why should it be illegal to sell something that's legal to give away? I can't follow the logic. Of all the things you can do to a person, giving them an orgasm is hardly the worst. In the army they give you a medal for killing people; in civilian life you go to jail for giving them orgasms. Am I missing something?

Wouldn't it be great if you could make a guy's head explode just by looking at him?

Guys don't seem to be called Lefty anymore.

JOIN THE RANKS OF THE UNCLEAN.

In someone else's house, when I sit on a warm toilet seat after seeing another person leave the bathroom, if that person was a man I'm not quite comfortable. But if it was a woman I feel just fine. Unless it was a really fat or old woman. Then it feels kind of creepy.

The reason I talk to myself is that I'm the only one whose answers I accept.

To my great disgust, the trend of naming children with what, until recently, had been considered surnames continues unabated. The latest abominations: Walker, Parker, Kendall, Flynn and McKenna. God help us.

Why aren't there any really disturbing pop songs, like "Tomorrow I'm Gonna Fuck Your Wife"?

If you were trying to clean up the world with a gun, you could sure do a lot worse than starting with a whole bunch of dead prosecutors.

I was thinking the other day that they ought to make those handicapped ramps a little steeper. And put a few curves in them, too. I could use some laughs.

Think of how entertaining it would be if all the people on TV still had their original teeth.

I think we ought to just go ahead and make "zillion" a real number. "Gazillion," too. A zillion could be ten million trillions, and a gazillion could be a trillion zillions. It seems to me it's time to do this.

A long time ago in England a guy named Thomas Culpepper was hanged, beheaded, quartered, and disemboweled. Why do I have the impression women were not involved in these activities?

I read somewhere that in Mexico City 300 tons of fecal matter are deposited in the air every day. So I guess you could say that not only does shit happen, it also falls on your head.

In Maine, in order to save energy, there are several lighthouses that are closed at night.

What's all the fuss about same-sex marriages? I've been the same sex all my life, and I was married for years. No problem. What's the big deal?

I think the best home security system of all would be one that locks the burglar inside his own house.

Sometime when you're watching a street musician, walk over in the middle of a song and whisper to him that you don't like his music. Then take a dollar out of his cup and walk away.

Sometime after John Denver's airplane crashed, a sheriff on TV was speculating that a pelican had flown into the plane. He actually said, "Birds are a hazard to aircraft." Funny, I always thought it was the other way around.

You know what's a fun thing to do? Go through your address book every few years and cross out the dead people.

If a group of people stand around in a circle long enough, eventually they will begin to dance.

Jesus doesn't really love you but he thinks you have a great personality.

Baseball entered its death throes when it began referring to fielding as "defense."

Have Some Fun: Walk into a gift shop and tell them you came in to get your gift.

Sony would be real smart to come up with a combination CD player and colostomy bag called the Shitman.

May I ask what all these grown men are doing walking around with fruity-looking backpacks? You see some goofy, twenty-eight-year-old yuppie wearin' a backpack. Like he's out prospecting for borax. What's in these packs that's so important? The nuclear launch codes? It's embarrassing. I don't know why I've allowed it to go on as long as I have.

I don't understand people who protest things in the street by walking around holding signs. I say, if you're gonna be on the street, use the time productively. Destroy some property.

How can it be a spy satellite if they announce on television that it's a spy satellite?

Why is it every time some celebrity gets cancer the *National Enquirer* says he's "vowed to lick this thing." Just once I'd like to hear a guy say, "I've got cancer, and this is it. I'll be dead in a few months."

Why don't they have a light bulb that only shines on things worth looking at?

Even though men are complete assholes, you know what makes me sad about feminism? Somewhere along the way we lost "Hey, toots!"

BRAVE NEW WORLD OF SCIENCE

* Scientists in Switzerland announced today they have been able to make mice fart by holding them upside-down and tapping them on the stomach with a ballpoint pen.

* A pair of Siamese twins in Australia, surgically separated six months ago, has been sewn back together. Apparently, each of them could remember only half the combination to their locker.

* Medical researchers have discovered a new disease that has no symptoms. It is impossible to detect, and there is no known cure. Fortunately, no cases have been reported thus far.

* The Nobel Prize in mathematics was awarded yesterday to a California professor who has discovered a new number. The number is "bleen," which he says belongs between six and seven.

* The surgeon general warned today that saliva causes stomach cancer. But apparently only when swallowed in small amounts over a long period of time.

* A Swedish entomologist claims that common houseflies are highly intelligent and can be trained to fix umbrellas and dance in a circle.

* Botanists in England have developed a plant that may help solve the world's hunger problems. Although it has no food value of its own, when the plant reaches maturity it sneaks across the yard and steals food from the neighbors.

* An x-ray technician at New York Hospital has died from a rare disease known as cancer-of-the-part-in-the-hair. In a desperate at-

tempt to treat himself, twenty-eight-year-old Norris Flengkt shaved his head completely bald. Unfortunately, the cancer thought it was simply a wider part and proceeded to devour his entire skull.

* Engineers at General Motors have developed a revolutionary new engine whose only function is to lubricate itself.

* Astronomers announced that next month the sun, the moon, and all nine planets will be aligned perfectly with the earth. They say, however, the only noticeable effect will be that the Nome to Rio bus will run four days late.

* Thanks to the sharp eyes of a Minnesota man, it is possible that two identical snowflakes may finally have been observed. While out snowmobiling, Oley Skotchgaard noticed a snowflake that looked familiar to him. Searching his memory, he realized it was identical to a snowflake he had seen as a child in Vermont. Weather experts, while excited, caution that the match-up will be difficult to verify.

* Geologists claim that although the world is running out of oil, there is still a two-hundred-year supply of brake fluid.

* According to astronomers, next week Wednesday will occur twice. They say such a thing happens only once every 60,000 years and although they don't know why it occurs, they're glad they have an extra day to figure it out.

* A team of microbiologists announced today they have discovered something they cannot identify. According to them it is long and thin and smells like a tractor seat.

IT'S NOT A SPORT

To my way of thinking, there are really only three sports: baseball, basketball, and football. Everything else is either a game or an activity.

Hockey comes to mind. People think hockey is a sport. It's not. Hockey is three activities taking place at the same time: ice skating, fooling around with a puck, and beating the shit out of somebody.

If these guys had more brains than teeth, they'd do these things one at a time. First you go ice skating, then you fool around with a puck, then you go to the bar and beat the shit out of somebody. The day would last longer, and these guys would have a whole lot more fun.

Another reason hockey is not a sport is that it's not played with a ball. Anything not played with a ball can't be a sport. These are my rules, I make 'em up.

Soccer. Soccer is not a sport because you can't use your arms. Anything where you can't use your arms can't be a sport. Tap dancing isn't a sport. I rest my case.

Running. People think running is a sport. Running isn't a sport because anybody can do it. Anything we can all do can't be a sport. I can run, you can run. For Chrissakes, my mother can run! You don't see her on the cover of *Sports Illustrated,* do you?

Swimming. Swimming isn't a sport. Swimming is a way to keep from drowning. That's just common sense.

Sailing isn't a sport. Sailing is a way to *get* somewhere. Riding the bus isn't a sport, why the fuck should sailing be a sport?

Boxing is not a sport either. Boxing is a way to beat the shit out of somebody. In that respect, boxing is actually a more sophisticated form of hockey. In spite of what the police tell you, beating the shit out of somebody is not a sport. When police brutality becomes an Olympic event, fine, then boxing can be a sport.

Bowling. Bowling isn't a sport because you have to rent the shoes. Don't forget, these are my rules. I make 'em up.

Billiards. Some people think billiards is a sport, but it can't be, because there's no chance for serious injury. Unless, of course, you welch on a bet in a tough neighborhood. Then, if you wind up with a pool cue stickin' out of your ass, you know you *might* just be the victim of a sports-related injury. But that ain't billiards, that's pool, and that starts with a *P*, and that rhymes with *D*, and that brings me to darts.

Darts could have been a sport, because at least there's a chance to put someone's eye out. But, alas, darts will never be a sport, because the whole object of the game is to reach zero, which goes against all sports logic.

Lacrosse is not a sport; lacrosse is a faggoty college activity. I don't care how rough it is, anytime you're running around a field, waving a stick with a little net on the end of it, you're engaged in a faggoty college activity. Period.

Field hockey and fencing. Same thing. Faggoty college shit. Also, these activities aren't sports, because you can't gamble on them. Anything you can't gamble on can't be a sport. When was the last time you made a fuckin' fencing bet?

Gymnastics is not a sport because Romanians are good at it. It took me a long time to come up with that rule, but goddammit, I did it.

Polo isn't a sport. Polo is golf on horseback. Without the holes. It's a great concept, but it's not a sport. And as far as water polo is concerned, I hesitate to even mention it, because it's extremely cruel to the horses.

Which brings me to **hunting.** You think hunting is a sport? Ask the deer. The only good thing about hunting is the many fatal accidents on the weekends. And, of course, the permanently disfigured hunters who survive such accidents.

Then you have **tennis.** Tennis is very trendy and very fruity, but it's not a sport. It's just a way to meet other trendy fruits. Technically, tennis is an advanced form of Ping-Pong. In fact, tennis is Ping-Pong played while standing on the table. Great concept, not a sport.

In fact, all racket games are nothing more than derivatives of Ping-Pong. Even **volleyball** is, technically, racketless, team Ping-Pong played with an inflated ball and a raised net while standing on the table.

And finally we come to **golf.** For my full take on golf, I refer you elsewhere in the book, but let it just be said golf is a game that might possibly be fun, if it could be played alone. But it's the vacuous, striving, superficial, male-bonding joiners one has to associate with that makes it such a repulsive pastime. And it is decidedly not a sport. Period.

GOLF COURSES FOR THE HOMELESS

War Is Heaven

When the United States is not invading some sovereign nation—or setting it on fire from the air, which is more fun for our simpleminded pilots—we're usually busy "declaring war" on something here at home.

Anything we don't like about ourselves, we declare war on it. We don't do anything about it, we just declare war. "Declaring war" is our only public metaphor for problem solving. We have a war on crime, a war on poverty, a war on hate, a war on litter, a war on cancer, a war on violence, and Ronald Reagan's ultimate joke, the war on drugs. More accurately, the war on the Constitution.

Be It Ever So Humble ...

But there's no war on homelessness. You notice that? It's because there's no money in it. If someone could end homelessness and in the process let the corporate swine steal a couple of billion dollars, you'd see the streets of America clear up pretty goddamn quickly. But if you think it's going to be solved through human decency, relax. It's not gonna happen.

You know what I think they ought to do about homelessness?

Change its name. It's not *home*lessness, it's *house*lessness. It's houses these people need. Home is an abstract idea; it's a setting, a state of mind. These people need houses. Physical, tangible structures. They need low-cost housing.

Get It Outta Here!

But there's no place to put it. People don't want low-cost housing built anywhere near them. We have a thing in this country called NIMBY: "Not in my backyard!" People don't want social assistance of any kind located anywhere near them. Just try to open a halfway house, a rehab center, a shelter for the homeless, or a home for retarded people who want to work their way into the community. Forget it. People won't allow it. "Not in my backyard!"

People don't want anything near them, especially if there's a chance it might help somebody. It's part of that great, generous American spirit we hear so much about. You can ask the Indians about that. If you manage to find one. We've made Indians just a little hard to find. Should you need more current data, select any black family at random. Ask them how generous America has been to them.

Lock the Bastards Up . . . Somewhere Else

People don't want anything near them. Even if it's something they think society needs, like prisons. Everybody says, "Build more prisons! But don't build them here."

Well, why not? What's wrong with having a prison in your neighborhood? It seems to me it would make for a fairly crime-free area. You think a lot of crackheads and thieves and hookers are gonna be hangin' around in front of a fuckin' prison? Bullshit! They ain't goin' anywhere near it.

What could be safer than a prison? All of the criminals are locked inside. And if a couple of them do manage to escape, what do you think they're gonna do? Hang around? Check real estate prices? Bullshit! They're fuckin' gone! That's the whole *idea* of breakin' out of prison: to get as far away as you possibly can.

"Not in my backyard." People don't want anything near them. Except military bases. They like that, don't they? Give 'em an army or a navy base; that makes 'em happy. Why? Jobs. Self-interest. Even if the base is loaded with nuclear weapons, they don't give a shit. They'll say, "Well, I don't mind a few mutations in the family if I can get a decent job." Working people have been fucked over so long, those are the kind of decisions they make now.

Putts for Putzes

But getting back to low-cost housing, I think I might have solved this problem. I know just the place to build housing for the homeless: golf courses. It's perfect. Plenty of good land in nice neighborhoods; land that is currently being squandered on a mindless activity engaged in by white, well-to-do business criminals who use the game to get together so they can make deals to carve this country up a little finer among themselves.

I'm sick of these golfing cocksuckers in their green and yellow pants, precious little hats, and pussified golf carts. It's time for real people to reclaim the golf courses from the wealthy and turn them over to the homeless. Golf is an arrogant, elitist game that takes up entirely too much space in this country.

Size Matters

The arrogant nature of golf is evident in the design and scale of the game. Think of how big a golf course is. It's huge; you can't see one end of it from the other. But the ball is only an inch and a half in diameter. So will someone please explain to me what these pinheaded pricks need with all that land?

America has over 17,000 golf courses. They average over 150 acres apiece. That's three million-plus acres. Four thousand, eight hundred and twenty square miles. We could build two Rhode Islands and a Delaware's worth of housing for the homeless on the land currently wasted on this meaningless, mindless, arrogant, racist game.

That's another thing: race. The only blacks you'll find in country clubs are carrying trays. And don't give me that Tiger Woods bullshit. Fuck Tiger Woods. He ain't black. He acts, talks, and lives like a white boy. Skin alone doesn't make you black.

Wake Me Up on the 19th Hole

And let's not forget how boring golf is. Have you ever watched it on television? It's like watching flies fuck. A completely mindless game. I should think it takes a fairly low intellect to draw pleasure from the following activity: hitting a ball with a crooked stick . . . and then walking after it! And then . . . hitting it again! I say, "Pick it up, asshole, you're lucky you *found* the fuckin' thing in the first place. Put it in your pocket and go the fuck home!" But, no. Dorko, in the plaid knickers, is gonna hit the ball again. And then he's gonna walk some more.

I say let these rich cocksuckers play miniature golf. Let 'em fuck with a windmill for an hour and a half. I wanna see if there's any real skill among these people. And yeah, yeah, I know there are plenty of golfers who don't consider themselves rich; people who play on badly maintained public courses. Fuck 'em! Fuck them and shame on them! Shame! For engaging in an arrogant, elitist, racist activity.

THE GOOD BREAD

When you make a sandwich at home, do you reach down past the first few slices to get the really good bread? It's a survival thing: "Let my family eat the rotten bread. I'll take care of Numero Uno."

And sometimes the issue isn't freshness but the size of the slice you're after. Everyone knows the wider ones are somewhere near the middle. So down you go past about six inferior slices to reach the ones you want. And, as you pull them up, you have to be careful they don't tear. Then, just before you get them out, the top six slices shift position and fall perpendicular to the rest of the loaf.

"Shit!"

I leave them that way. Let the family think a burglar made a sandwich.

SHORT TAKES

Did you notice that several years ago everything got different?

I never read memoirs; the last thing I need is someone else's memories. I have all I can do to deal with my own.

It takes two scales to find out how much a scale weighs.

In this era of "maxi," "mega" and "meta," you know what we don't have anymore? "Super-duper." I miss that.

Fuck whole-grain cereal. When I want fiber, I eat some wicker furniture.

Suggestions I ignore: "George, you go out and draw their fire, I'll sneak up on them from behind."

You men, next time a prostitute solicits your business, ask for the clergymen's rate.

I think doctors, who must always remain emotionally detached, should be accompanied on their hospital rounds by peasant women from the Middle East. The ones who cry and wail and throw themselves on coffins at those terrorist funerals you see on television. Just for balance.

The only thing high-definition television will do is provide sharper pictures of the garbage.

Have you noticed that some companies now call their menial employees "associates"? They're trying to make them feel better in spite of subsistence salaries. "Associates" is a very slippery job title. Don't be fooled by it.

God bless the homicidal maniacs. They make life worthwhile.

There are patriotic vegetarians in the American Legion who will only eat animals that were killed in combat.

Peg Leg Bates Jr.'s sole ambition was to follow in his father's footstep.

When I was a kid I can remember saying, "Cross my heart and hope to die." I'd like to confess now that I never really meant the second part.

Very few Germans know that in honor of her husband, Mrs. Hitler combed her pussy hair to one side.

You don't hear a lot from imps anymore.

FECES TAKE PLACE

I think TV remotes should have a button that allows you to kill the person on the screen.

The phrase "digging up dirt" seems wrong. If you use a shovel correctly, the very first time you stick it in the ground the thing you come up with is dirt. The dirt is right there on top. It doesn't have to be "dug up."

When you're at someone else's house, and they leave you alone in a room, do you look in the drawers? I do. I'm not trying to steal anything; I just like to know where everything is.

I don't understand this notion of ethnic pride. "Proud to be Irish," "Puerto Rican pride," "Black pride." It seems to me that pride should be reserved for accomplishments; things you attain or achieve, not things that happen to you by chance. Being Irish isn't a skill; it's genetic. You wouldn't say, "I'm proud to have brown hair," or "I'm proud to be short and stocky." So why the fuck should you say you're proud to be Irish? I'm Irish, but I'm not particularly proud of it. Just glad! Goddamn glad to be Irish!

Don't you think it's funny that all these tough-guy boxers are fighting over a purse?

I wonder: On rainy nights, does the sandman send the mudman?

I think they ought to have an annual ceremony at the White House called the Bad Example Award. They should give it to the one person in America who has made the most complete disaster of his own personal life. Someone who through drugs or alcohol or simply a bad attitude has been fired, arrested, killed a marriage, completely alienated friends and family, and perhaps even attempted suicide several times. But it must have happened because of personal behavior and conscious choices, not bad luck. It seems to me people like that never receive any recognition.

Christian deodorant: "Thou Shalt Not Smell"

Lou Gehrig was a pretty tough guy, but I wonder how he handled it when they told him he had Lou Gehrig's disease.

Most people don't know what they're doing, and a lot of them are really good at it.

Sea World should have a special aquarium that features fish sticks. In fact, I wouldn't mind seeing Mrs. Paul herself swimming around in there: "Hi, kids!"

Do you think Sammy Davis ate Junior Mints?

Have you noticed when you wear a hat for a long time it feels like it's not there anymore? And then when you take it off it feels like it's still there? What is that?

I can never decide if "what's-his-name" should be capitalized.

Do you know why they call it a blow *job*? So it'll sound like there's a work ethic involved. Makes a person feel like they did something useful for the economy.

As soon as someone is identified as an unsung hero, he no longer is.

It isn't generally known, but you can save money on phone calls by simply not letting the other person talk. Studies have shown that on many phone calls as much as 50 percent of the talking is done by the other person. If you can manage to dominate the conversation, you can save money.

DYING TO STAY ALIVE

You're all going to die. I hate to remind you, but it is on your schedule. It probably won't happen when you'd like; generally, it's an inconvenience. For instance, you might have your stamp collection spread out on the dining room table.

[Ominous music]

"Now?"

"Now."

"May I at least put away my commemoratives?"

"No."

Inconvenient.

Nobody wants to die. Nobody. Well, maybe Evel Knievel, but most other people don't like the idea. It doesn't seem like an enjoyable thing. People figure if being sick is no fun, dying must really be a bother. After all, part of the pleasure of being alive is the knowledge that you're not dead yet.

And when you get right down to it, people don't mind *being* dead, it's getting dead that bothers them. No one wants to *get* dead. But we're all gonna do it. Death is one of the few things that are truly democratic—everybody gets it once. But *only* once. That's what makes us nervous. No rehearsals.

TICKET TO NOWHERE

And actually, I think people should look forward to death. After all, it's our next big adventure. At last we're going to find out where we go. Isn't that what we've all been wondering? Where we go?

"Where do we go?"

"I don't know."

"We must go somewhere."

"True."

"Phil says he knows."

"I know he does. But take my word, Phil doesn't know."

Where do we go? Maybe it's nowhere; that would be interesting. On the one hand, you'd be nowhere, but on the other hand, you wouldn't know it. So at least you'd have something to think about. Or not.

Personally, I think we go wherever we *think* we're going to go. What you think is what you get. Have you ever heard one of those guys who says, "Don't even bother prayin' for me, I'm goin' straight to hell; I'm goin' to hell to be with all my friends"? Well, he is. He's going to hell, and he'll probably be with all his friends. What you think is what you get. If you keep saying you're going to heaven, chances are you'll get there. But don't look for any of your friends.

In my own case, I expect I'll be going to a public toilet in Honduras. And by the way, should you be interested, I can tell you on good authority that when Monty Hall dies he will be spending a lot of time behind door number three.

DEATH: THE SHOW

Die Big

My feeling is that as long as you're going to die, you should go out with a bang. Make a statement. Don't just "pass away." Die!

"Arnie passed away."

"He did?"

"Yes. Quietly, in a chair."

"I didn't know."

"Well, that's the idea; no one knows."

"True. On the other hand, they say Jim *died*."

"Oh, yes, Jim died! He died, and now he's dead! He had a thirty-minute seizure in a hotel, danced across the lobby, and wound up in a fountain, twitching uncontrollably. Bellhops were actually applauding."

"God bless him, he went out big."

I say go out big, folks; it's your last chance to make a statement. Before you go, give 'em a show; entertain those you leave behind.

Two-Minute Warning

Now, you might be wondering why I would even suggest that someone can affect the manner and style of his death. Well, it's because of a mysterious and little-known stage of dying, the two-minute warning. Most people are not aware of it, but it does exist. Just as in football, two minutes before you die you receive an audible warning: "Two minutes! Get your shit together!" And the reason most people don't know about it is because the only ones who hear it are dead two minutes later. They never get a chance to tell us.

But such a warning does exist, and I suggest that when it comes, you use your two minutes to entertain and go out big. If nothing else, deliver a two-minute speech. Pick a subject you feel passionate about, and just start talking. Begin low-key, but, with mounting passion, build to a rousing climax. Finally, in the last few seconds, scream at those around you, "If these words are not the truth, may God strike me dead!" He will. Then simply slump forward and fall to the floor. Believe me, from that moment on, people will pay more attention to you.

Of course, such a speech is not your only option; circumstances may permit a more spectacular exit. Perhaps you'll get your two-minute warning during an aerobics class. If so, volunteer for something strenuous. Grab three sets of dumbells, strap on a lot of leg weights, and start running on the treadmill at a really steep grade. When they tell you to stop, turn the treadmill up to 20 miles an hour and start leaping in the air. Tell them it's a new exercise called the Hindu Death Leap. Then collapse on the treadmill, allowing it to fling you backward into the mirrored wall, breaking the mirror and showering everyone with small pieces of glass. I guarantee the police will search your locker carefully.

"Heal This!"

Or maybe you'll be lucky enough to receive your two-minute warning while attending Christian faith-healing services. This is a wonderful opportunity to give religion a bad name. After the sermon, when they ask for those to come forward who "need a miracle," stand up and get on line with the cripples. Try to time things just right. Cut into line if you have to. Then, with barely ten seconds left, kneel in front of the preacher. He will place his hands on you, shout, "Heal!" and you will croak at his feet. Not quite a miracle, but certainly an attention-getter. And the nice thing is they'll blame it on the preacher:

THOUSANDS LOOK ON AS EVANGELIST SLAYS WORSHIPER. POLICE STUDY VIDEOTAPE.

Posthumous Fun

But you needn't be satisfied with merely an impressive death scene. You can actually take it a bit further, past the moment of death, by preprogramming some posthumous reflexes into your brain. Remember, the central nervous system runs on electricity, and dying takes place in stages. So, not all of your electrical energy is fully discharged at the time you are pronounced dead; some of it remains stored. Morgue and funeral workers report that corpses often spasm and twitch as much as two days after death.

So I say, as long as you have that potential, be creative. Before you die, try using autosuggestion and visual imaging to preprogram into your brain a few posthumous reflexes. Things that will entertain the folks you leave behind and capture their imaginations. You might want to consider humming during your autopsy, or snapping your fingers during the embalming, or—always a big winner at a wake—bolting upright in your coffin and screaming, "I'm not really dead!" That one is especially fun if someone has brought along impressionable children.

But perhaps you're of a more conservative stripe. If so, at your wake, something as simple as squeezing off several dozen loud but artistically redeeming farts might bring a smile to the faces of those who knew you best: "Isn't that just like Uncle Bob," they'll chuckle, as they rush to open a window.

So, folks, I think my message is clear: even in death, obligations to your loved ones do not end. You still have the responsibility to entertain and ease their grief. And should you persist, and be truly creative with these postdeath efforts, you may accomplish the rare feat of leaving behind a group of incensed relatives who beat you with heavy clubs until they are satisfied that you're fully and completely dead.

FUNERALS

I don't like to attend funerals. When I die, I don't want a funeral, because I'm sure of one thing: if I don't like other people's funerals, I'm going to hate my own.

And I don't want a wake. I don't like the idea of lying on display, dead, in a mahogany convertible with the top down. Everybody looking, and you're dead. They have no idea you're wearing short pants, and have no back in your jacket. It's embarrassing. Especially if they use too much makeup, and you look like a deceased drag queen.

And as you're lying there half-naked, one by one they kneel down and stare silently into your coffin. It's supposed to look reverent. What they're really doing is subtracting their age from yours to find out how much time they have left. That is, if they're younger. If they're older, they just gloat because you died first.

"He looks good."

"Dave, he's dead."

"I know. But when he was alive he didn't look this good."

It's a perverse fact that in death you grow more popular. As soon as you're out of everyone's way, your approval curve moves sharply upward. You get more flowers when you die than you got your whole life. All your flowers arrive at once. Too late.

And people say the nicest things about you. They'll even make things up: "You know, Jeff was a scumbag. A complete degenerate scumbag. But he meant well! You have to give him that. He was a complete degenerate well-meaning scumbag. Poor Jeff."

"Poor" is a big word when discussing the dead.

"Poor Bill is dead."

"Yeah, poor Bill."

"And poor Tom is gone."

"Jeez, yeah, poor Tom."

"Poor John died."

"Poor John. Hey, what about Ed?"

"Ed? That motherfucker is still alive! I wish he would die."

"Yeah. The dirty prick. Let's kill him."

JUST FOR FUN

When writing a letter of reference for a friend, give him a glowing recommendation, but just for fun, conclude by saying, "Don't let Dave's legal history trouble you. There's reason to believe the little girl was lying."

Just for fun, knock on the door of any stall in a public rest room and say, "Sir! Please try to control the smell in there. Don't force us to bring in the hoses."

Call one of those How-Am-I-Driving 800 numbers and, just for fun, complain about a particular driver. Tell them he was driving on the sidewalk, vomiting, giving the finger to old women, and dangling a baby out the window.

Next time you're at a baseball game, sing the national anthem in a loud voice, but just for fun, alternate each line between English and complete gibberish:

O-oh say can you see,
Floggie bloom skeldo pronk,
What so proudly we hailed,
Clogga dronk slern klam dong blench.

See if that doesn't get the fans talking among themselves.

While strolling past a sidewalk café, just for fun, squeeze off several truly repulsive farts, silent or noisy. If silent, stand to one side and watch the results; if noisy, tip your hat and say, "Bon appetito."

Walk through a crowded amusement park carrying a small tape recorder that plays the sound of a little girl's voice screaming, "Help, Mommy, the man is touching me like Daddy does at home!" Just for fun.

SHORT TAKES

When you step on the brakes your life is in your foot's
hands.

Attending college at a place called Bob Jones University is like putting
your money in Nick & Tony's Bank.

I think what the authorities need is a SQUAT team. Here's how it would work: A squad of
heavily armed police break into the house and take a shit in the living room.

Burma is now called Myanmar, Ceylon is Sri Lanka, and Upper Volta is
Burkina Faso. How can they do that? How can they just change the
name of a country? It doesn't seem right to me.

The Jews are smart; they don't have a hell.

No one ever says "half a week," although obviously there is such a thing.
As in, "I'll be back in a week and a half."

FUCK RATIONAL THOUGHT

You know who would make an interesting murder—suicide?
Madeleine Albright and Yanni.

When they print the years of someone's birth and death, can you resist figuring out how old they were?

I hope reincarnation is a fact so I can come back and fuck teenagers again.

Let me tell you something, if we ever have a good, useful, real-life revolution in this country, I'm gonna kill a whole lot of motherfuckers on my list. For purposes of surprise, I'm not revealing the names at this time.

If a centipede wants to kick another centipede in the shins, does he do it one leg at a time? Or does he stand on fifty of his legs and kick with the other fifty?

McDonald's says "100 Billion Served." Bullshit, they hand them to you. There's a difference.

SPOTS ARE DOTS UP CLOSE.
DOTS ARE SPOTS FAR AWAY.

Why is it a pile of dirty clothes is called "the laundry"? "I'm about to do the laundry." And then, when it comes out of the machine, it's still called "the laundry"? "I just did the laundry." What's the deal here? Is laundry clean or dirty?

The reason county fairs don't have kissing booths anymore is because someone noticed that a lot of the men in line had hard-ons.

Wouldn't you like to read some of the things they found in the suggestion box after a meeting of the Aryan Brotherhood?

This year for the Oscars and Emmys I wore my usual outfit: filthy underwear. I enjoy television a lot more when I'm comfortably dressed.

Regarding "safe and sound": I've often been safe, but seldom have I been thought of as sound.

True Stuff: There is actually an auto race called the Goody's Headache Powder 500.

I think Kleenex ought to put a little bull's eye right in the middle of the tissue. Wouldn't that be great? Especially when you're hangin' out with your buddies: (KNNERRFFF! SNGOTT!) "Look, Joey, an 85!"

Dusting is a good example of the futility of trying to put things right. As soon as you dust, the fact of your next dusting has already been established.

What exactly is a wingding?

When Thomas Edison worked late into the night on the electric light, he had to do it by gas lamp or candle. I'm sure it made the work seem that much more urgent.

Have you noticed that in the movies lately a popular thing to do is stick someone's head in the toilet and flush the toilet repeatedly? Where did that come from? They never used to do that. You never saw Spencer Tracy stick Henry Fonda's head in the toilet. Maybe Katharine Hepburn's, but not Henry Fonda's.

A stone's throw is much farther than a hop, skip, and a jump, but it's not nearly as far as a whoop, a holler, and a stomp.

Amusement parks should have a ride where people are pursued by the police at high speed, and when they're caught they're beaten and tortured.

When you think about it, attention deficit disorder makes a lot of sense. In this country there isn't a lot worth paying attention to.

Why do they call one sport "women's tennis," and then turn around and call the other one "ladies' golf"?

Once a year they should have No Hairpiece Day. So everyone could see what all these baldy-headed, fake-hair jerkoffs really look like.

Who decides when the applause should die down? It seems like it's a group decision; everyone begins to say to themselves at the same time, "Well, okay, that's enough of that."

I'm tired of these one-sided heavyweight fights. I think Mike Tyson should just go ahead and fight a leopard. At least it would be an even match. And I wish he would bite more people. God, that was great. I think it would be fun if he just started biting people on the street for no reason.

As a child, I used to wonder if Charlie McCarthy had little wooden balls.

ADVENTURES IN THE SUPERMARKET

Have you ever selected an item in the supermarket and put it in some-one else's cart? Then you realize what you're doing and you get sort of an alien feeling?

"Wait! This is not my cart. Look at this! Brown flour and sheep entrails. God, I almost put my capers in this cart. Where's mine? Oh, there it is! The one with the tapioca cupcakes and the mango popsicles. Thank God."

Or have you ever started to walk off with someone else's cart?

"Hey! That's my stuff!"

You have to think fast. "Not yet it isn't! It's not paid for. Tech-nically, these things still belong to all of us. And if I feel like shopping out of your cart, that's what I'll do. Let's see, any organic scallions in there? What's this? Elk milk? That'll be just fine. You may leave now."

I've found the best way to shop for food is to work up a really big appetite. Fast for several days, smoke a couple of joints, take $700 . . . and go to the supermarket! It's great. You buy everything!

"Wow, canned bread! Just what I need!"

And all the good things, the things you really love and can't do without? Well, you buy two of them, because you know you're going to eat one of them on the way home at a red light.

Shopping hungry is great; you just keep loading things into your cart. But then, after several aisles, you realize you may have overdone it: You find yourself pushing a motorcade of three carts, all tied together with long loops of string cheese. Once again, you've lost control.

And so, as you realize you don't have enough money to pay for everything, you begin to put back some of the more expensive items. Like meat.

"Meat? Twenty-seven dollars? Bullshit! I'll put back these steaks and grab a few more pound cakes. The kids shouldn't be eating meat, anyway."

The nicest thing about putting things back in the supermarket is that you can put them anywhere you want. No one cares. You can leave the Robitussin next to the ham hocks and stick the marshmallows in with the Bacon Bits. They don't care. They have people who come around at midnight to straighten that stuff out, and in the morning everything is back where it belongs.

By the way, next time you shop at a supermarket in a neighborhood that has higher than average marijuana use, take a look at the cookie section. Combat zone. Half the packages have been opened, and all the really good cookies are gone.

"Where the hell are the Mallomars?"

"Oh, we can't get Mallomars into the store. Folks line up at the loading dock for Mallomars."

There are always plenty of crappy cookies. You ever notice that? Shitty, low-priced local cookies? Like "Jim's Home-Style Cookies. Twenty-six varieties." I say, "Damn, Jim, if you can't make cookies in twenty-five tries leave me out."

Time to head home, folks. Let's get on the checkout line here and read *People* magazine. By the way, I must admit I'm a real sucker on the checkout line. I'm an impulse buyer. Anything that's on display, I want it. I even buy things other people leave behind.

"Wow! Extra spicy diet fudge raisin tartar sauce. Must be a sale. Great. I got the last one!"

One last thought: have you ever been on the express line and tried to convince the tough-looking Hispanic girl with the tattoos that twenty-seven packages of hot dogs are really just one item? I'm always grateful when she finally gives in. "Go ahead, mister, it's quicker than beating the shit out of you."

WELL, AT LEAST THE PLATE WAS BLUE

I often wonder why there's no blue food. Every other color is well represented in the food kingdom: corn is yellow, spinach is green, raspberries are red, carrots are orange, grapes are purple, and mushrooms are brown. So where's the blue food?

And don't bother me with blueberries; they're purple. The same is true of blue corn and blue potatoes. They're purple. Blue cheese? Nice try. It's actually white cheese with blue mold. Occasionally, you might run across some blue Jell-O in a cafeteria. Don't eat it. It wasn't supposed to be blue. Something went wrong.

FUSSY EATER

When I was a kid, I was a fussy eater. That's what they called it at our house.

"He's a fussy eater."

"Fussy eater" is a euphemism for "big pain in the ass." They'd trot out some food, and I'd say, "I don't like that."

"Why?"

"I don't know. I know I don't *like* it. And I know that if I ate it, I would like it even less."

"Well, I like it. Mmmmm! Yum yum!"

"Hey, Ma. You like it? You eat it!"

Sometimes they would try to corner me with logic: "Well, how do you *know* you don't like it, if you've never even tried it?"

"It came to me in a dream." Big pain in the ass.

Some things I didn't like because of the way they sounded.

"Don't sound right to me, Ma. Say that again?"

"Asparagus."

"No, I don't like that." Imagine. I got away with that for eight or nine years.

To this day, there are still some things I won't eat because of how they sound. Yogurt sounds disgusting. I can't eat anything that has both a "y" and a "g" in it. Squash is also badly named.

"You want some squash?" Sounds like someone sat on dinner.

"How would you like a nice tongue sandwich? It's made from slices of a cow's tongue."

"Hey, Ma, are you fuckin' tryin' to make me sick?"

There are also foods that sound too funny to eat. Like guacamole. It sounds like something you yell when you're on fire. "Holy guacamole! My ass is burnin'!"

Or when you can't remember the name of something. "Ed, where's that little guacamole that plugs into the lamp?"

Another food too funny to eat: garbanzo beans. Sounds like acrobats. "Ladies and gentlemen, from Corsica, the fabulous Garbanzos!"

On the other hand, there were some foods I didn't like because of how they *looked*. That seems a bit more rational.

"I don't like that! It don't look right to me. Did you make that, Ma? Yeah? Is there a picture of it in the cookbook? I'll bet it don't look like *that*."

Of course, some people will eat anything, no matter how it looks. I saw guys like that on the chow line in the army.

"Hi, boys! Whaddaya got? I'll eat anything. What's that called? Never mind, gimme a whole bunch of it."

"It's rat's asshole, Don."

"Well, it sure makes a hell of a fondue."

Not me. I don't eat anything I don't recognize immediately. If I have to ask questions, I pass. I'm not at dinner to make inquiries. Gimme somethin' I recognize. Like a carrot. I know I can trust a carrot.

Now, there are some foods that even though I know what they are, I still don't like their looks. Tomatoes, for instance. My main problem with tomatoes is that they don't look as though they're fully developed. They look like they're still in the larval stage; thousands of tiny seeds and a whole lot of jelly-lookin' slime. "Get it off my plate! It's slimy!" It's like that stuff at the end of an egg.

Of course, I know it's not the end of an egg . . . it's the beginning of a chicken!! "It's hen come! Eeeeaaaaghhh! Get it off my plate!"

Oh, I'm fun in the coffee shop.

Lobsters and crabs don't look like food to me, either. Anything with big pinchers crawling toward me sideways doesn't make me hungry. In fact, my instinct is "Step on that fuck! Step on him before he gets to the children!"

And I definitely cannot eat oysters. Not for the usual reason— their similarity to snot—but because when I look at the whole oyster I think, "Hey, that's a little house. Somebody lives in there. I'm not gonna break in on a guy just to have a meal. He might be making a pearl. Maybe he just brought home a do-it-yourself pearl kit and cleared off the dining room table. Who am I to interfere with the plans of an oyster?"

RUNNING HOT AND COLD

The refrigerator butter warmer is a strange invention. Originally, humans were cold so they built a warm enclosure. A house. Cold outside, warm inside the house. Everything was fine until they realized that inside the warm enclosure the meat tended to spoil. So they built a cold enclosure—a refrigerator—inside the warm enclosure. Warm in the house, cold in the refrigerator. Everything was fine until they realized that inside the cold enclosure the butter got too hard to spread. So they built an even smaller warm enclosure—a butter warmer—inside the cold enclosure, which was already inside the larger warm enclosure. Strange.

ICEBOX MAN

Around our house I'm known as Icebox Man. One of my duties is keeping people from standing too long with the icebox door open while they decide what to eat. You know, someone smokes three joints and decides to inventory the refrigerator. Drives me crazy.

"Close the fuckin' door, will ya? You're letting out all the cold. Here's twenty dollars, go down to the Burger King! I'll save that much on electricity. Close the goddamn door! If you can't decide what you want, take a Polaroid picture, go figure it out, and come back later. You kids are lucky. We didn't have Polaroids, we had to make an oil painting."

I try not to let them get me down, though, because Icebox Man has an even bigger job: picking through the refrigerator periodically, deciding which items to throw away. Most people won't take that responsibility; they grab what they want and leave the rest. They figure, "Someone is saving that; sooner or later it'll be eaten." Meanwhile the thing, whatever it is, is growing smaller and denser and has become permanently fused to the refrigerator shelf.

Well, folks, Icebox Man is willing to make the tough decisions. And I never act alone; I always include the family.

"I notice some egg salad that's been here for awhile. Are we engaged in medical research I haven't been told about?"

"May I assume from the color of this meat loaf that it's being saved for St. Patrick's Day?"

"Someone please call the museum and have this onion dip carbon-dated."

"How about this multihued Jell-O from Christmas? It's July now. If no one wants this, I'm going to throw it away."

Did your mother ever pull that stuff on you? Offer you some food that if you didn't eat it she was "Just going to throw it away"? Well, doesn't that make you feel dandy?

"Here's something to eat, Petey. Hurry up, it's spoiling! Bobby, eat this quickly; the green part is spreading. If you don't eat it, I'm going to give it to the dog." It's so nice to be ahead of the dog in the food chain.

Icebox Man has had some interesting experiences. Have you ever been looking through the refrigerator and come across a completely empty plate? Nothing on it but a couple of food stains? It's unnerving. I think to myself: "Could something have eaten something else? Maybe the Spam ate the olives. Maybe that half-eaten chicken isn't really dead. He's living on *our* food." Sometimes I picture a little mouse in a parka, hiding behind the mustard, waiting for the refrigerator light to go off so he can resume his cold-weather foraging.

Probably the worst experience is reaching into the refrigerator and finding something you simply cannot identify at all. You literally do not know what it is. It could be meat; it could be cake. At those times, I try to bluff.

"Honey? Is this good?"

"What is it?"

"I don't know! I've never seen anything like it. It looks like, well, it looks like . . . meat cake!"

"Smell it!"

"It has no smell whatsoever."

"That means it's good! Put it back. Someone is saving it for something." That's what frightens me; that someone will consider it a challenge and use it in soup. Simply because it's there.

It's a leftover. What a sad word: leftover.

But think about this. Leftovers make you feel good twice. First, when you put them away, you feel thrifty and intelligent: "I'm saving food!" Then, a month later, when blue hair is growing out of the ham, and you throw it away, you feel *really* intelligent: "I'm saving my life!"

DOG MOMENTS #3

Big Dog, Little Dog

Dogs come in all sizes. There are lots of little dogs, and lots of big dogs. And when I say big dogs, I don't mean just big dogs. I mean BIG, FUCKIN', HUGE GODDAMN DOGS! Some people got huge dogs that look more like livestock. Dogs that oughta be wearin' commercial license plates.

"What the hell is that?"

"That's my dog."

"Jesus, man, he blocked out the sun!"

"That's Tiny. He's a Great Alaskan Horse Moose Dog. Say 'hello,' Tiny. No, no! Tiny! Put the man down! Bad dog!"

Little dogs are different. Little dogs jump all around, and their legs move real quick. They got those teeny little legs. They got legs that if you feel around under the fur it's like a pepperoni stick under there.

Sometimes they jump up high. Some of 'em can jump clear up onto a real high bed.

[Boing!]

"Holy shit, what a jump! Lemme see ya do that again."

Put him back on the floor.

[Boing!]

"God, I can't believe it. C'mon, one more time."

Back onto the floor.

[Boing!]

And I make him keep doin' it and doin' it, over and over, until he gets all tired out and can't quite reach the bed anymore. I let him fall short a few times and crash back onto the floor. Then and only then, if I decide I *want* him on the bed, I put him up there myself. It's my decision; I buy the dog food.

Fleeky Disappoints

Besides, if you *do* allow him on the bed, sooner or later he'll create an incident. Before the evening is over, he will force one of the humans to turn to the other and say,

"Honey, did you fart?"

"Not me. I thought *you* farted."

"Not me! Phewww! That's not even one of my farts! I told you, I've got four farts. My Heineken's fart, my broccoli fart, my rice pudding fart, and my nondairy creamer fart. And the fart I'm smellin' right now is definitely not one of mine."

[Sniffing]

"Wait a minute. I know! The dog farted!! Fleeky farted! Fleeky, why did you fart? Look at him! Look how guilty he looks. He knows he farted. I seen his asshole open up. I seen it. What? Well, I just happened to be lookin' at his asshole by chance, that's all. What kind of a question is that? I was simply glancin' at his asshole, and I saw it open up. I thought he was doin' some kinda deep-breathing exercise. I had no idea he was into chemical warfare."

SHORT TAKES

I don't mind leaving my house as long as I don't have to look at a lot of unattractive Americans in the process. Visors, logo hats, fat thighs, beer bellies, bad haircuts, halter tops, cheap sneakers, camcorders, and unattractive children wearing blank expressions. God, these people are ugly. I stay home a lot.

I always refer to any individual member of the Red Sox as a Red Sock. Is this correct?

America: where the Irish, English, Germans, Scandinavians, Poles, and Italians all came together to kill Indians, lynch niggers, and beat the shit out of spics and Jews.

Next guy who says to me, "Badda-boom, badda-bing," is gettin' kicked right in the fuckin' nuts.

I was one of the people at Woodstock who took the brown acid. Lemme tell ya, there was nothing wrong with it.

NEVER FORGET, HITLER WAS A CATHOLIC.

Here would be a good epitaph for some guy: "I want everyone to know it was great being alive, and I really enjoyed myself. I especially enjoyed fucking and going to the movies."

If you listen to his voice carefully without looking at the screen, Ted Koppel sounds like he's taking a shit.

There's a thing called shaken-baby syndrome that people get upset about. Personally, I think you have to give 'em a good shake, or they don't bake uniformly.

The Golden Gate Bridge should have a long bungee cord for people who aren't quite ready to commit suicide but want to get in a little practice.

If a movie is described as a romantic comedy you can usually find me next door playing pinball.

Somehow I enjoy watching people suffer.

My most frequent sex fantasy: to work in a delicatessen and have a woman come in and ask me to give her a pound of tongue.
>   And I'd say, "Well, I don't get off till four o'clock."
>   And she'd say, "Well, I don't get off at all, that's why I want some tongue."

If they decide to cover Viagra under Medicare, we'll all be paying for other people's hard-ons.

You know what they ought to have? Motherfucker's Day. The day after Mother's Day ought to be Motherfucker's Day. Actually, when you think about it, Father's Day is Motherfucker's Day.

Attention men: The dumb-looking shaved-head thing has finally played out. Try finding some other way of pretending to be cool and different.

In applying the stereotype that all old people are slow-thinking and dull-witted, what's often overlooked is that many of these people were slow-thinking and dull-witted throughout their lives. At this point they're simply older versions of the same unimpressive people.

My main operating principle: Don't take any shit from the zeitgeist.

History is not happenstance; it is conspiratorial. Carefully planned and executed by people in power.

The mayfly lives only one day. And sometimes it rains.

You know what you never hear about anymore? Quicksand. When I was a kid, movies and comic books had quicksand all the time. What happened? Same thing with whirlpools. You never hear about some guy being sucked down into a whirlpool anymore. I miss that.

I think they ought to have black confetti. It would be great for funerals. Especially if the dead person wasn't too popular.

If you really want to put a faith healer to the test, tell him you want a smaller shoe size.

You never seem to get laid on Thanksgiving. I think it's because all the coats are on the bed.

In the United States, anybody can be president. That's the problem.

You know how you can tell when a moth farts? When he suddenly flies in a straight line.

Do you realize that somewhere in the world there exists a person who qualifies as the worst doctor? If you took the time, by process of elimination you could actually determine the worst doctor in the world. And the funny part is knowing that someone has an appointment to see him tomorrow.

I often think of something my grandfather used to say. He'd tell me, "I'm goin' upstairs and fuck your grandma." He was a really honest man. He wasn't going to bullshit a five-year-old.

Just beyond the edge of the solar system, in the Oort Cloud, there's a swarm of about a trillion comets orbiting the sun. Let's hope that right now one of them is turning slightly and pointing itself directly at Mississippi.

The police in Los Angeles said recently that some man had been stabbed in the San Pedro area. Believe me, I know how painful that can be; I was once bitten there by a dog. It's especially painful when you go to the bathroom.

Doesn't Jonesboro sound to you like a place where everyone has a drug habit?

DOG MOMENTS #4

Gimme a New One

I love my dog. I love *all* my dogs. Every dog I ever had, I still love 'em. And in my life, believe me, I have had me a bunch of goddamn dogs. Because you keep on gettin' a new one, don't ya? It's true. As life goes on, you keep gettin' one new dog after another. That's the whole secret of life. Life is a series of dogs.

Sometimes you can get a dog that looks exactly like the one you had before. It's true. If you shop around a little, you can find you a dog identical to your former dog. You just bring the dead one into the pet shop, throw him up on the counter, and say, "Gimme another one of these." And, by God, they'll give you a carbon copy of your ex-goddamn dog. And that's real handy, because then you don't have to go around your house changin' all the pictures.

That's the nice thing about dogs. They don't live too long, and you can go and get a new one.

Doggie Nose Best

Most people know the best size dog to have is a knee-high, midsize dog. It's the ideal pet. Because whenever some nice lady comes to visit you, the first thing that dog does is put his nose right in her crotch.

"Hi, Mrs. Effington."

"Hi, Stuart, how's the . . . oooooh! Ooooooh! What a friendly dog. Oooohhhh! You know, I'll bet he smells *my* dog."

"I'm not sure, Mrs. Effington. Judgin' by where he's placed his nose, I'd say he's got a completely different animal in mind. You don't by any chance own a pussy, do ya?"

"No. I mean . . . well, no!"

Some people get embarrassed by that nose-crotch behavior. The dog owner will often fall all over himself trying to save face.

"Stop that, Bongo! Stop it! I'm awfully sorry, Marzell. He's usually so polite. You musta not bathed."

Not me, folks; I never apologize. I'm a fun-lovin' guy. I say, "Get in there, Bongo! Get yourself some of that. Sniff it out. Listen, Marzell, would you mind spreadin' your legs a little bit, so he can get some sniffin' room? Plant your feet about three feet apart, would ya? That's it. Good. Air that thing out. Okay! So, how's everything goin' down at the church? Good. All right, Bongo, now go around back and sniff that other thing. Sorry, Marzell, there's two smells he likes, and one of 'em's in the back. What's that? You gotta go? Well, I'm awfully sorry. Listen, before you go, you wouldn't be willin' to let Bongo have about thirty seconds on your leg, would ya? No, I didn't think so. Okay, no problem. You take care, and tell the reverend Bongo says hello."

Those dogs are really great. They help to break the ice when a new neighbor comes to call.

"Hi, we're the Belchingtons. Ooooooh! What's his name?"

"Ballsniffer. He's a crotch hound. Lemme know if you wanna get circumcised; he's on duty 'round the clock."

Give the Little Dog a Big Hand

When they show a dog on TV, do you try to get your dog to look at him? Don't you want your dog to see the dog on TV? I do.

"Look at the doggie! Look at the dog! Over there! On TV! Look!"

He won't look. Even if you try to twist his head around and point it toward the TV, he won't look.

"Over there! Turn your head! Look! On TV! Look at the dog! Goddamn it, you asshole! Look at the fuckin' dog!!"

They never look where you want. If you point at something, they just stare at your hand. You try to show them something interesting, and they think you're showing them your hand.

"There he goes again, showing me his hand. Why does he do that? I guess he's really proud of it. Uh-oh! Now he's twisting my head around. Owww! Jeez, what did I do now?"

"Well, for one thing you completely missed the dog on TV."

A Cracker Jack Meal

A long time ago I had a little dog named Tippy. And one time when I was doin' drugs, I fed Tippy a whole bunch of Cracker Jack, because that's what I was havin'. Cracker Jack and tap water. Seemed like a reasonable meal to me. And even though Tippy was a little dog, she ate about two boxes of Cracker Jack. And the next day, when I took her out for a walk, she squatted and strained and grunted and shook, and you know what? By God, instead of taking a shit, she took a Cracker Jack! Right in front of my eyes I saw fully formed, undigested Cracker Jack coming out of my dog!

Well, you know me, I'm a practical guy. I kept waitin' for the little surprise to come out, hopin' it wouldn't be a whistle or a bird call. I figure there's a certain amount of basic hygiene you can't ignore.

NOT EXACTLY MARTHA STEWART

Did your dog ever eat a whole bunch of brightly colored balloons, and when he took a shit it turned out to be real festive looking? Or maybe at Christmas he'd eat some tinsel off the tree and take a dump near the manger, and it would glisten with light from the yule log, filling your heart with Christmas spirit? Isn't it great?

Dogs are a constant source of entertainment. Did you ever have a dog who ate cat turds? Some of them do. Some dogs will eat cat turds. Of course, you gotta have a cat; you can't be goin' down to the supermarket and buyin' cat turds.

But it's true. Sometimes a dog will eat cat turds. Don't let him lick your face that day. Get him a bottle of Listerine, and make him gargle. Pour it down his throat and tell him to howl. Then you can let him lick you.

One more thing about dog chow, and this includes a little household hint that'll help you keep your lawn neat and clean. Feed your dog rubber bands. Just mix ten or eleven rubber bands in with his food. He won't care. He'll eat anything as long as it's mixed in with something he likes.

Feed him a bunch of rubber bands, and then when he takes a shit, you'll notice there's a handy little rubber loop stickin' out of one end of the turd. Then, all you gotta do is pick up the loop, swing that turd around, and throw it in the next yard. Tell your neighbor it's a new thing: flying lawn food.

HAVE A NICE DAY

I don't have nice days anymore. I don't bother with that. I'm beyond the nice day; I feel I've outgrown the whole idea. Besides, I've already had my share of nice days. Why should I be hogging them all? Let someone else have a few.

Naturally, everyone still *wants* me to have one. Every person I meet wants me to have a nice day. Especially clerks.

"Have a nice day."

"Yeah, yeah, yeah. You wanna gimme my fuckin' change, please? I'm triple-parked!"

Some of them are really insistent.

"I said have a nice day! Do it!"

"All right, all right! I'll give it a shot."

That's the trouble with "Have a nice day." It puts all the pressure on you. Now you have to go out and somehow arrange to have a positive experience. All because of some loose-lipped clerk.

Have a nice day, indeed! Maybe I don't *feel* like having a nice day. Maybe—just maybe—I've had twenty-seven nice days in a row, and I'm ready for a crappy day. You never hear that, do you?

"Have a crappy day!"

"Why, thank you. Right back at ya! And to your wonderful family as well!"

A crappy day; that would be easy. No trouble at all. No planning involved. Just get out of bed and start moving around.

I think what bothers me most about the whole "nice day" thing is that word "nice." It's a weak word. It doesn't have a lot of character. Nice.

"Isn't he nice? He is so nice. And she's nice too! Isn't that nice? How nice they are!"

I don't care for it. It's like "fine." Another weak word.

"How are you?"

"Fine."

Bullshit! Nobody's fine. Hair is fine.

"How's your hair?

"Fine."

That makes more sense to me.

Some guys are "great"! You ever meet those guys?

"This is great! Isn't this great? Goddamn, this is great! Look, they're gonna kill that guy! Isn't that great?"

Not me. I'm not nice, I'm not fine, I'm not great. People ask me how I am, I don't give them any superlatives; nothing to gossip about. I tell them I'm "fairly decent." Or "relatively okay." I might say, "I'm moderately neato." And if I'm in a particularly jaunty mood, I'll tell them, "I'm not unwell, thank you."

That one always pisses them off. Because they have to figure it out for themselves.

HELLO-GOODBYE

We have so many ways of saying hello. Howdy, hi there, how are ya, how ya doin', how's it goin', how do ya do, what's new, what's goin' on, whaddaya think, whaddaya hear, whaddaya say, whaddaya feel, what's happenin', what's shakin', que pasa, what's goin' down, and what it is?

You know my favorite? "How's your hammer hangin'?" That's a good one, isn't it? Doesn't work too well with women, though. Unless you're talking to a lady carpenter. Then it's perfectly acceptable.

I've always wanted to use that one on a high church official.

"Good evening, Your Holiness. How hangs thy hammer?"

So far, I haven't had the opportunity.

There's one form of saying hello that bothers me. It's when a guy says, "Are they keepin' you busy?" It's like he thinks someone has the right to come around and give me odd jobs.

Whenever a guy says, "Are they keeping you busy?" I always tell him, "Well, your wife is keeping me pretty busy!" And that seems to hold him for about a half an hour.

Of course, we also have many ways to say good-bye. Bye-bye, so long, see you later, ta-ta, be cool, take it easy, stay loose, hang in, take care, and keep on truckin'. You know my favorite? "Don't get run over." Well, I find some people need practical advice.

Occasionally, someone will say to me, "Have a good one!" I just laugh and say, "I already have a good one. Now I'm looking for a *longer* one!" And that seems to hold them for about a half an hour.

Then there are all the foreign ways we say good-bye. Some people when they leave you, they think they have to get fancy. They whip an "arrivederci" on you. Or an "au revoir." Some guys say, "adios." Or the American version, "Adios, motherfucker!"

In Hawaii they say, "aloha." That's a nice one. It means both "hello" and "good-bye." Which just goes to show, if you spend enough time in the sun you don't know whether you're coming or going.

Do you ever get in a rut with your manner of saying good-bye and find yourself using the same phrase, over and over? And you begin to feel a little stupid?

For instance, if you're leaving a party, and you have to say good-bye to five or six people standing in a group, you say, "Okay, hey, take it easy. Okay, hey, take it easy. Okay, hey, take it easy. Okay, hey, take it easy. Okay, hey, take it easy. Okay, hey, take it easy." And you feel like a goddamn moron.

You know what I do? Every month, whether I need to or not, I change the way I say good-bye; I start using a different phrase. People like that. They notice that little extra effort. They'll say to me, "Pardon me, but didn't you used to say 'Okay, hey, take it easy'?"

And I say, "Yes I did. But not anymore. Now I say, 'Farewell! Farewell, till we meet again. May the forces of evil become confused on the way to your house!' " That's a strong one, isn't it? People will remember you if you talk like that.

Sometimes, for a joke, you can combine several ways of saying good-bye that don't seem to go together. Like "Toodle-oo, go with

God, and don't take any wooden nickels." Then people don't know *what* the fuck you're talking about.

Or you can choose to say good-bye in a realistic manner. "So long, Steve. Don't let self-doubt interfere with your plans to improve your life."

Well, some people need practical advice.

LOVE AND REGARDS

Have you noticed that quite often when you leave someone they ask you to relay an affectionate message to someone else? They'll say, "Give my love to Klaus. Tell Klaus Rebecca sends her love."

Do you mind that? Do you mind being used that way? The awesome responsibility of carrying Rebecca's love to Klaus? Suppose you don't see Klaus? What do you do with Rebecca's love? Carry it around? Give it to someone else?

"Wilhelm! I can't find Klaus, here's some of Rebecca's love."

Suppose Wilhelm doesn't know Rebecca? Can he legally accept her love? Especially when it was originally intended for Klaus?

Or suppose you give Wilhelm Rebecca's love for Klaus, and then you run into Klaus, what do you give him? All you had was Rebecca's love, and you've already gone and given that to Wilhelm. Can you reasonably ask Wilhelm to give back Rebecca's love? Maybe he's gotten used to it by now. Can Klaus sue Wilhelm? Can Wilhelm be arrested? Can *you* be arrested for transporting love across a state line?

All right, back to reality. Just for the sake of argument, let's leave Wilhelm out of this altogether. Suppose Rebecca gives you her love to give to Klaus, and you *do* see Klaus, what form should the love take? Can you risk giving Klaus a tongue kiss? Which brings up another possibility: maybe Klaus is gay. Klaus doesn't *want* Rebecca's love, Klaus wants *Wilhelm's* love! If Klaus tells you to give his love to Wilhelm, just tell him, "Bullshit, Klaus. You give your *own* love to Wilhelm. I'm going to find Rebecca!"

Now, sometimes people don't quite want you to give their love to someone else; they only want you to give their "regards." That's all they're sending that day. Regards. That's not as important as love, is it? No. By the way, do you always relay the type of affection the sender intends? I don't. Generally, I wait till the last minute and then decide what the other person deserves.

For instance, Susan might say to me, "Give my love to Dave." Well, I might not feel Dave is deserving of Susan's love. Dave might be one of those people who piss me off. I'll probably just give him a few regards; keep him in his place. I feel it's my decision. After all, I'm the one who's doing all the work.

And if I *really* don't like the recipient, I might reduce the level of affection by an even greater degree. Susan might say, "Give all my love to Dave and tell him I can't wait to see him again so I can hold him in my arms, kiss his sweet, soft lips, and make love to him all night." And I'll say, "Dave! Susan says hello." Screw Dave! That's what he gets for pissing me off.

Then there are the recipients who try to anticipate what degree of affection they're going to receive.

"Did Susan send her love?"

"No, Dave. She only sent her regards."

"That's funny, usually she sends her love."

"Well, not this time. In fact, she specifically told me, 'Don't give Dave any of my love.' It seems she's running short of love and has to be careful whom she gives it to. However, she did say she's overstocked with regards and wants you to have a whole bunch of them. So, be satisfied, Dave. Take your regards, and get the fuck out of my life!"

Well, he should damn well be satisfied with regards; it's a lot better than simply being sent someone's "best." There are some people who just send you their best.

"Give my best to Dave."

"Your best what, Susan? If this is your best, perhaps you'd better keep it to yourself."

And yet, receiving someone's "best" is better than simply being "remembered to," isn't it? That's the lowest of all. Hardly worth even telling the poor person.

"Remember me to Dave."

"Okay."

"Dave? You remember Susan?"

"Yes."

"Well, she remembers you, too."

That's it, my job is done. I'm off now to find Tex, so I can tell him Billy Bob said "Howdy."

One final thing. There are times when someone wants you to convey more than simply love. They want you to give someone "a big hug and kiss." Now they've got you trafficking in sex.

"Give Joachim a big hug and a kiss for me."

Usually it's women. I find that women are a bit more expressive at times like these. And sometimes they're really explicit.

"Bye-bye, Elena. Drive carefully. Give Flaco a nice blow job for me. And don't forget to lick his asshole!"

"Okay, Belinda. But next time let's get Klaus to take care of that!"

EXPRESSIONS I QUESTION

There are many expressions we take for granted. We use them all the time, yet never examine them carefully. We just say them as if they really made sense.

Legally drunk. Well, if it's legal, what's the problem? "Leave me alone, officer, I'm legally drunk!"

You know where you can stick it. Why do we assume everyone knows where they can stick it? Suppose you don't know? Suppose you're a new guy, and you have absolutely no idea where you can stick it? I think there ought to be a government booklet entitled *Where to Stick It*. Now that I think of it, I believe there *is* a government booklet like that. They send it to you on April 15.

Undisputed heavyweight champion. Well, if it's undisputed, what's all the fighting about? To me, "undisputed" means we all agree. Here you have two men beating the shit out of one another over something they apparently agree on. Makes no sense.

It's the quiet ones you gotta watch. Every time I see a television news story about a mass murderer, the guy's neighbor always says, "Well, he was very quiet." And someone I'm with says, "It's the quiet ones you gotta watch."

This sounds like a very dangerous assumption. I'll bet anything that while you're busy watching a quiet one, a noisy one will kill you.

Suppose you're in a bar, and one guy is sitting over on the side, reading a book, not bothering anybody. And another guy is standing up at the front, bangin' a machete on the bar, screamin', "I'm gonna kill the next motherfucker who pisses me off!"

Who you gonna watch?

Lock him up and throw away the key. This is one you hear a lot from men. Men like to talk that way; it makes 'em feel tough. A guy sees a rapist on the TV news, he says, "You see that guy? They oughta lock him up, and throw away the key."

This is really stupid. First of all, every time the guy's gotta take a shit, you're gonna have to call the locksmith. If he's in prison thirty years, even if he's eatin' government cheese, it's gonna cost you a fortune.

Second, where do you throw the key? Right out in front of the jail? His friends'll find it! How far can you throw a key? Fifty, sixty feet the most. Even if you hold it flat on its side and scale it, whaddaya get? An extra ten feet, tops! This is a stupid idea that needs to be completely rethought.

Down the tubes. That's one you hear a lot. People say, "This country is goin' down the tubes." What tubes? Have you seen any tubes? Where are these tubes? And where do they go? And how come there's more than one tube? It would seem to me for one country all you need is one tube. Does every state have to have its own tube? One tube is all you need.

But a tube that big? Somebody would have seen it by now. Somebody would've said, "Hey Joey! Lookit the fuckin' tube! Big-ass fuckin' tube, over here!" You never hear that. You know why? No tubes! We don't have tube one. We are, sorry to say, tubeless.

Takes the cake. "Boy, he really takes the cake." Where? Where do you take a cake? To the movies? You know where I would take a cake? Down to the bakery, to see the other cakes. And how come he takes the cake? How come he doesn't take the pie? A pie is easier to carry than a cake. "Easy as pie." A cake is not too hard to carry, either. "Piece of cake."

The greatest thing since sliced bread. So this is it? A couple of hundred thousand years . . . sliced bread? What about the Pyramids? The Panama Canal? The Great Wall of China? Even a lava lamp, to me, is greater than sliced bread. What's so great about sliced bread? You got a knife, you got a loaf of bread. Slice the fuckin' thing!! And get on with your life.

Out walking the streets. This is another one you hear from men. Some guy sees a rapist on the news. Same rapist as before; only this time he's being released. The guy says, "You see that? You see that guy? They're lettin' him go! Now, instead of bein' in prison, he's out walkin' the streets!"

How do we know? How do we know he's out walkin' the streets? Maybe he's home bangin' the baby-sitter. Not everybody who gets a parole is out walkin' the streets. A lot of times they steal a car. We oughta be glad. "Thank God he stole a car. At least he's not out walkin' the streets."

Fine and dandy. That's an old-fashioned one, isn't it? You say to a guy, "How are ya?" He says, "Fine and dandy." Not me. I never say that. You know why? Because I'm never both those things at the same time. Sometimes I'm fine. But I'm not dandy. I might be close to dandy. I might be approaching dandy. I might even be in the general vicinity of dandyhood. But not quite fully dandy. Other times, I might indeed be highly dandy. However, not fine. One time, 1978. August. For about an hour. I was both fine and dandy at the same time. But nobody asked me how I was. I coulda told 'em, "Fine and dandy!" I consider it a lost opportunity.

Walking papers. Some guy gets fired, they say, "Well, they gave him his walkin' papers today." Lemme ask you something. Did you ever get any walking papers? Seriously? Believe me, in my life I got fired a lot of times. I never got any walkin' papers. I never got a pink slip, either. You know what I would get? A guy would come around to my desk and say, "Get the fuck outta here!!" You don't need paper for that.

The riot act. They keep saying they're going to read that to you. Tell the truth, have you heard this thing at all? Ever?

It's especially a problem when you're a kid. They like to threaten you.

"You wait'll your father comes home. He's gonna read you the riot act!"

"Oh yeah? Well, tell him I already read it myself! And I didn't like it! I consider it wordy and poorly thought out. If he wants to read me somethin', how about *The Gentleman's Guide to the Golden Age of Tongue-Kissing?*

More than happy. I'll bet you say that sometimes. I'll bet you say, "Oh, I'd be more than happy to do that." How can you be more than happy? To me, this sounds like a dangerous mental condition. "We had to put Laszlo under physical restraint; he was . . . well, he was more than happy."

One more of these expressions: **In your own words.** You hear it in classrooms. And courtrooms. They'll say, "Tell us . . . in your own words . . ." Do you have your own words? Personally, I'm using the ones everybody else has been using. Next time they tell you to say something in your own words, say, "Nigflot blorny quando floon."

SHORT TAKES

I don't hear much of that elevator music anymore. What's going on?

IT'S TIME TO START SLAPPING PEOPLE

Don't you think there were probably a lot of singers with great voices who never got famous because they were too ugly to stand up and be seen in public?

I can't wait to see one of those actor-assholes who drive race cars get killed on TV.

Why do women wear evening gowns to nightclubs? Why don't they wear nightgowns?

I think many years ago an advanced civilization intervened with us genetically and gave us just enough intelligence to develop dangerous technology but not enough to use it wisely. Then they sat back to watch the fun. Kind of like a human zoo. And you know what? They're getting their money's worth.

After you die, your "stuff" becomes your "personal effects."

GOD BLESS US ALL. RIGHT IN THE MOUTH

I think people should be allowed to do anything they want. We haven't tried that for a while. Maybe this time it'll work.

People ask me if I have an e-mail address, and I say, "www.fuckyou.com@blowme/upyourass." And they seem to understand.

Message to the Denver Nuggets regarding Columbine High School: There's no reason to cancel a sporting event just because some kids kill each other. Try to concentrate on basketball and leave the life-and-death shit to someone else.

Capitalism tries for a delicate balance: It attempts to work things out so that everyone gets just enough stuff to keep them from getting violent and trying to take other people's stuff.

Baseball bats are now the preferred weapon for many drug gangs and others who have a business need to administer behavioral reminders. They're cheap, lethal, legal, untraceable, and hey! It's the national pastime.

Dying must have survival value. Or it wouldn't be part of the biological process.

Why is it that, when making reference to something in the past, people often think they have to say, "I hope I'm not dating myself"? Listen, if you're so embarrassed by your age there's a simple solution: open a vein.

I don't have hobbies, I have interests. Hobbies cost money. Interests are free.

With all the presidential administrations we've had, I'm sure that by now there must have been at least one person who, besides being in the cabinet, was also in the closet.

I don't like it when I'm in an audience and the emcee tells us to give someone a welcome specific to that city: "Let's all get together and give this little lady a nice Toledo welcome." I've often thought if I were from Toledo it would be fun now and then to give someone a Baltimore welcome, just to break the emcee's balls. Or maybe slip in an exotic Budapest welcome when no one is expecting it. One thing I would never do is give someone a Dallas welcome. That's what JFK got. Dallas welcomes don't last too long.

You rarely see an elderly midget. Apparently their life spans are shorter too.

A PEAR IS A FAILED APPLE

You keep hearing that society's greatest tasks are educating people and getting them jobs. That's great. Two things people hate to do: go to school and go to work.

We busy ourselves with meaningless gestures such as Take Our Daughters to Work Day, which applies primarily to white, middle-class daughters. More help for the wrong people.

People seem to think that if there's some problem that makes them unhappy in this country, all they have to do is stage a big march and everything will change. When will they learn?

Complaint: Where did this dumb-ass Sammy Sosa thumping-your-chest, kissing-your-fingers, flashing-the-peace-sign nonsense come from? What's that stupid shit all about? Geraldo does a variation on it. It strikes me as pretentious, meaningless, pseudoreligious bullshit.

I don't know about you, but I really have no problem with atrocities. What's the big deal? Lighten up.

Can placebos cause side effects? If so, are the side effects real?

When hundreds of people are killed in an airplane crash I always wonder if maybe there wasn't one guy, a little behind schedule that day, who ran down the last few hundred yards of the airport concourse to make the plane on time. And when he finally sat down in his seat, out of breath, he was really glad he made it. And then an hour later the plane goes down. What goes through his mind? Do you think maybe in those last few moments, as he plunges to the Earth he wishes he'd had a heart attack while running through the airport?

Why do they bother with a suicide watch when someone is on death row? "Keep an eye on this guy. We're gonna kill him, and we don't want him to hurt himself."

I notice at Jewish weddings they break a glass. You ever been to an Irish wedding? Glasses, bottles, mirrors, tables, chairs, arms, legs, the band instruments, and the groom's neck. We don't fuck around. Mazel tov!

HOW SOON IS INTERMISSION?

I recently attended an avant-garde play. Here's what it said in the program:

An Anteater, a Tire Iron and a Blue Hat
by Zal Fenchley

Act One

SCENE 1 Laura's living room, several weeks later.

SCENE 2 Easter, aboard a Turkish woman's thigh.

SCENE 3 Deep within the colon of a woolly mammoth. 16,376 B.C.

SCENE 4 Inside a sailor's shorts during the attack on Pearl Harbor.

Act Two

SCENE 1 On a French sidewalk, six feet from escargot vomit.

SCENE 2 Inside a condom in Haifa. Jewish New Year.

SCENE 3 At your aunt's house. Soon.

Act Three

SCENE 1 In a Shriner's hatband following oral sex.

SCENE 2 Down where Arturo used to live. Not that long ago.

Act Four

John Lennon two songs. (not tonight)

HAVE A GOOD TIME

You know what bothers me? People who want to know the time. The ones who come up and ask me, "What time is it?" as if I, personally, were responsible for keeping track of such things.

Sometimes they phrase it a little differently. They'll say, "Do you have the time?" And I say, "No. I don't believe I do. I certainly didn't have it this morning when I left the house. Could you possibly have left it somewhere? You know, now that you mention it, I believe the navy has the time. In Washington. They keep it in an observatory or something, and they let a little of it out each day. Not too much, of course. Just enough. They wouldn't want to give us too much time; we might not use it wisely." Sometimes, in a playful mood, when asked if I have the time, I'll say, "Yes," and simply walk away.

When Is It, Anyway?

I do that because I hate to disappoint people. You see, there is no time. There's just no time. I don't mean, "We're late, there's no time." I mean, there is no time.

After all, when is it? Do you know? No one really knows when it is. We made the whole thing up. It's a human invention. There are no numbers in the sky. Believe me, I've looked; they're not there. We made the whole thing up.

So, when are we? Sometimes we think we know *where* we are, but we really don't know *when* we are. For all we know, it could be the middle of last week.

And the time zones are no help; they're all different. In fact, in parts of India the time zones actually operate on the half hour instead of the hour. What is that all about? Does anybody really know what time it is?

What Year Do You Have?

And never mind a piddly little half-hour difference in India, how about thousands of years? The major calendars disagree by thousands of years. To the Chinese, this is 4699; the Hebrews think it's 5762; the Muslims swear it's 1422. No telling what the Mayans and Aztecs would say if they were still around. I guess their time ran out.

Remember, folks, these are *calendars* we're talking about, instruments specifically designed to keep track of time. And they're all different. And they're not just off by a couple of weeks, this is thousands of goddamn years we're talking about. How did that happen?

Our current (Gregorian) calendar is such an amateur show that every four years we have to cram in an extra day just to make the whole thing work. We call it February 29. Personally, I don't believe it. Deep down, I know it's really March 1. I mean, it just *feels* like March 1, doesn't it?

But even that simple quadrennial adjustment doesn't fix things, so every 100 years we suspend that rule and dispense with the extra day. Unless, of course, the year is divisible by 400, in which case we suspend the suspension and *add* the extra day. But that's still not quite enough, so every 4,000 years we suspend that rule too, and back comes February 29!

Here's how we got to this sorry state: The Julian calendar was introduced in 46 B.C., the Roman year 709, but it was off by eleven minutes a year, so by 1582 there was an accumulated error of ten days. Accordingly, that year Pope Gregory XIII decreed that the day following October 4 would be called October 15. They just skipped ten days. Threw them out. Officially, in 1582, no one was born in France, Italy, Spain or Portugal during the period October 5 through October 14. Weird, huh?

But even weirder, Britain didn't adopt the Gregorian calendar till

1752, when they dropped eleven days out of September. Since this also applied to the American colonies, officially, no one was born here from September 3 through September 13, 1752. Except Indians. By the way, during that same year New Year's Day was moved from March 25 to January 1. The way it had been handled before, for example, was that March 24, 1750, would be followed by March 25, 1751. Pretty fucked up, huh? And you thought that big millennium party you went to was being held right on time.

Staying in the "Now"

We try hard to keep track of time, but it's futile. You can't pin it down. For example, there's a moment coming . . . it's not here yet . . . it's still in the future . . . it's on the way . . . it hasn't arrived . . . it's getting closer . . . here it is . . . Oh shit, it's gone!

We use words like "now." But it's a useless word, because every time you say it, it means something different.

"Can you tell me the time?"

"Which time did you want? Now? Or the time you asked me? Or how about now? Is this the time you want? Speak up, this stuff isn't standing still."

And think of the phrase "just now."

"Did you hear that?"

"What?"

"Just now."

"You mean, 'Just then.' "

"Yes, just then. Wait, there it is again!"

"When?"

"Just now."

Everything we think of as "now" is either the very recent past or the very near future. There's no present. "Welcome to the present." ZOOM! Gone again!

Keep It Vague

It's all so imprecise that people sometimes don't bother with minutes and hours at all; they keep things purposely vague.

"What time you got?"

"Just after."

"Just after? Jeez, my watch is slow. I got 'goin' on.' "

It's amazing how something as precisely calibrated as time can be described so loosely. Especially where short periods of time are concerned. We say "at once," "immediately," "right away," "just like that," "no time at all," "nothing flat," "at a moment's notice."

And one that I never understood: "Before you can say Jack Robinson." You don't hear that much anymore, do you? Maybe Jack ran out of time. Maybe he was an Aztec.

And let's not forget a "jiffy." Or a "flash." Do you know which is quicker? Well, I looked it up; in fact, there are two jiffies in a flash. And there are six flashes in the twinkling of an eye. No one seems to know how many twinklings of an eye there are in two shakes of a lamb's tail. And, by the way, why is it *two* shakes of a lamb's tail? Wouldn't the basic unit of measurement be one shake of a lamb's tail?

All of a Sudden

Another vague word is "soon." For me, soon has an emotional quality; it has great potential for sadness.

"Is Daddy ever coming to visit us again?"

"Yes."

"When?"

"Soon."

Here's a spooky one: "Sooner than you think." Wow! Sooner than I think. That's like "before you know it."

"I'll be back before you know it."

ZOOM!

"Holy shit! He did it!!"

"Sooner or later," "one of these days," "any day now," "from time to time," "every now and then," "a little while."

"A little while" is nice. So gentle. "I'll be home in a little while." That wouldn't bother you, would it? I think anyone could wait a little while. It doesn't sound too threatening.

"Your father is sick, but he still has 'a little while.' " That's different from "a short time." A short time sounds terminal.

"Your father has only a 'short time.' "

If I were about to be executed, I'd much rather have a little while than a short time.

A Good Time

By the way, do you have a favorite period of time? It isn't easy to select a favorite period of time, there are so many appealing ones. I have a few.

To me, the most useful period of time is five minutes. That seems to be the one most people choose when they're pressed. "I'll be there in five minutes." "Give me five minutes, will ya?" "Whattaya, kiddin'? I could fix that thing in five minutes!"

That's all most people want. Five minutes. A good, solid, respectable period of time. And it goes by fast. I think I could do just about anything for five minutes. Even the most distasteful task.

"Let's go talk to George Bush."

"Are you kiddin'? He's an asshole."

"Look, just five minutes, okay?"

"Okay, five minutes. But no more! After that I'm gonna puke."

Fifteen minutes is a popular period of time. But it has an institutional ring to it. A regulatory quality. It sounds like it's associated with something either compulsory or forbidden.

"The exchange window will only be open for fifteen minutes."

"You have fifteen minutes to fill out the forms . . ."

"In fifteen minutes we will be coming around and . . ."

I like twenty minutes better. Twenty minutes sounds kind of free and sporty.

"I'll be back to pick up those test papers in fifteen minutes. Then you'll have a twenty-minute break."

"Hey guys, cover me with the boss, will ya? I'll be back in twenty minutes."

Twenty minutes. Just enough time to get laid.

Have a good time.

SHORT TAKES

Why was brown excluded from the rainbow? And where did indigo come from? I was taught there were three primary colors and three secondary colors. What's with this indigo shit?

After the hurricane is gone, where do people put all that plywood?

Standing ovations have become far too commonplace. What we need are ovations where the audience members all punch and kick one another.

Watching television these days, I often wonder what happened to the "vertical hold" knob. I miss that.

Don't you hate when a rock band comes onstage and apparently the drummer has decided that somehow it's cool to wear a funny hat?

There's a store near my house with a sign that says, Unfinished Furniture. I must go in there. I'm looking for a nice three-legged table.

If you live long enough, everyone you know has cancer.

I once was dancing with a woman who told me she had a yeast infection. So I asked her to bake me a loaf of bread.

Why don't these people who live in hurricane-prone areas just keep some batteries on hand at home? Seems like a simple thing to me. There's too much last-minute shopping.

I'm always relieved when someone is delivering a eulogy and I realize I'm listening to it.

Why don't network TV shows have a warning that says "Caution: You are about to watch a real piece of shit." Actually, they could just leave it on the screen all the time.

All music is the blues. All of it.

I think it would be interesting if old people got anti-Alzheimer's disease where they slowly began to recover other people's lost memories.

Electricity is really just organized lightning.

You know what they ought to have on planes? A passenger voice recorder. So we could hear all the screaming when a plane goes down. I'm not really interested in the cockpit recorder; the pilots are always talkin' a bunch of technical shit anyway. But the passengers! That would be fun.

When you rub your eyes real hard do you see that checkerboard pattern? What is that?

"Coming soon to a theater near you." Actually, there is no theater near you. Look around your street. Is there a theater near you?

Attention certain women: Transporting children is not a license to drive slowly.

I saw a sign that said, Coming Soon—a 24-Hour Restaurant. And I thought, Well, that's unusual. Why would they open and close it so quickly? At least try it for a week or two, and see if you can build a clientele.

Why is it when the two main characters in an action movie have their big climactic fight it always turns out that both of them are really good fighters? Just once, wouldn't you like to see a fight between two leading male characters where one of them gets the shit completely beat out of him in about eight seconds? Especially the hero.

I've noticed my flax bill is not too high.

Would someone please explain to me the supposed appeal of having grandchildren? People ask me, "Are you a grandfather yet?" as if it's some great thing. I'm sure it has its charms, and I imagine some dull-witted people want to see their genes passed along just for the sheer novelty of the idea. But overall, I don't get it.

It's been on my mind for some time, but I've never said it publicly. So here goes: "Vo-do-de-o-do and a scoddie-woddie doo-dah day." Thank you.

Boy, am I glad to finally be rid of that fuckin' Mother Teresa.

Masturbation is not illegal, but if it were, people would probably take the law into their own hands.

It used to be you got a tattoo because you wanted to be one of the few people who had a tattoo. Now you get a tattoo because you don't want to be one of the few people who don't have a tattoo.

Just when I discovered the meaning of life, it changed.

People in Washington say it's not the initial offense that gets you in trouble, it's the cover-up. They say you should admit what you did, get the story out, and move on. What this overlooks is the fact that most of the time the cover-up works just fine, and nobody finds out a thing. I would imagine that's the rule rather than the exception. My advice: Take a chance. Lie.

The IQ and the life expectancy of the average American recently passed each other going in opposite directions.

Hotel fun: Smoke a big fat joint and then watch a complex spy movie with a lot of characters and plot twists. Then a few weeks later at a different hotel, smoke another joint and watch the same movie. It's like seeing a whole new film. But the real fun is that about every fifteen minutes something happens in the plot that you seem to know already. It's an odd feeling. By the way, this exercise can probably be repeated indefinitely with the same movie. As long as the grass holds out.

This is just one more way of starting a sentence with the word "this" and ending it with the word "that."

Odd Slang: A woman who fucks a priest is said to have "taken a ride on the holy pole."

PEOPLE I CAN DO WITHOUT

* Guys in their fifties named Skip.

* Anyone who pays for vaginal jelly with a platinum credit card.

* An airline pilot wearing two different shoes.

* A proctologist with poor depth perception.

* A pimp who drives a Ford Escort.

* A gynecologist who wants my wife to have three Quaaludes before the examination.

* Guys with a lot of small pins on their hats.

* Anyone who mentions Jesus more than 300 times in a two-minute conversation.

* A dentist with blood in his hair.

* Any woman whose hobby is breast-feeding zoo animals.

* A funeral director who says, "Hope to see you folks again real soon."

* A man with only one lip.

* A Boy Scoutmaster who works at a dildo shop.

* People who know the third verse to the "Star Spangled Banner."

* Any lawyer who refers to the police as "the federales."

* A cross-eyed nun with a bullwhip and a bottle of gin.

* Guys who have their names printed on their belts.

✳ A brain surgeon with BORN TO LOSE tattooed on his hand.

✳ Couples whose children's names all start with the same initial.

✳ A man in a hospital gown, directing traffic.

✳ A waitress with a visible infection on her serving hand.

✳ People who have large gums and small teeth.

✳ Guys who wear the same underwear until it begins to cut off the circulation to their crotch.

✳ Any woman whose arm hair completely covers her wristwatch.

CANCER IS GOOD FOR YOU

A lot of people worry that their drinking water isn't safe, because it contains things that cause cancer. Not me. I don't care if the water is safe or not, I drink it anyway. You know why? Because I'm an American, and I expect a little cancer in my water. I'm a loyal citizen and I'm not happy unless government and industry have poisoned me a little every day.

Besides, cancer never hurt anybody. People need a little cancer. It's good for you; it keeps you on your toes. I ain't afraid of cancer, I had broccoli for lunch. Broccoli kills cancer. A lot of people don't know that. It's not out yet.

It's true. You find out you got some cancer, get yourself a fuckin' bowl of broccoli. That'll wipe it right out. Cauliflower, too. Cauliflower kills the really big cancers, the ones you can see from across the street through heavy clothing. Broccoli kills the little ones, the ones that are slowly eating you away from inside. While your goofy, half-educated doctor keeps telling you, "You're doin' fine, Jim."

In fact, bring your doctor a bowl of broccoli, he's probably got cancer, too. Probably picked it up from you. They don't know what they're doing. It's all guesswork in a white coat. What you gotta try to do is develop more than one kind of cancer, so you can turn 'em against one another. That's what you gotta hope for: that the cancers eat each other up instead of you. Fact is, the way I look at it, the more cancer you got, the healthier you are.

THE HUMOROUS SIDE OF RAPE

Many people in this country want to tell you what you can and can't talk about. Or sometimes they'll tell you you can talk about something, but you can't joke about it. Like rape. People say you can't joke about rape. They say rape's not funny. And I say, Fuck you, I think it's hilarious. How do you like that? I can prove rape is funny: Picture Porky Pig raping Daisy Duck. See? Hey, why do you think they call him Porky?

And I know what men are gonna say. Daisy was askin' for it; she was comin' on to Porky, she had on tight feathers. Porky got horny, and he lost control. A lot of men talk like that. They blame it on the woman. They say, "She had it comin'. She was wearing a short skirt."

Doesn't seem fair to me; doesn't seem right. But I believe you can joke about it. I believe you can joke about anything. It just depends on how you construct the joke, what the exaggeration is. Every joke needs one exaggeration. Every joke needs one thing to be way out of proportion.

I'll give you an example. Have you ever seen a news story like this? Some burglar breaks into a house, steals some things, and while he's in there, he rapes an eighty-one-year-old woman. And you think to yourself, "Why? What the fuck kind of social life does this guy have?" I want to ask him, "Why did you do that?" But I know what I'd hear: "Hey, she was comin' on to me. She had on a tight bathrobe." And I'm thinkin', "Next time, be a little more selective, will you?"

Now, speaking of rape, but changing the subject slightly, you know what I wonder? Is there more rape at the Equator or the North Pole? I mean, per capita; I know the populations are different. I think it's the North Pole.

Most people think it's the Equator. Because it's hot down there, people don't wear a lot of clothing, guys can see women's tits, they get horny, and there's a lot of rape and a lot of fucking in general. But that's exactly why there's *less* rape at the Equator; because there's a lot of fucking, in general. You can tell the Equator has a lot of fucking; look at the population figures. Billions of people live near the Equator. How many Eskimos we got? Thirty? Thirty-five?

No one's gettin' laid at the North Pole; it's too cold. An Eskimo says to his wife, "Hey, honey, how about some pussy?" She says, "Wally, are you crazy? The windchill is 150 below!" Eskimo guys are deprived, they're horny, they get pent up, and every now and then they gotta rape somebody.

Now, the biggest problem an Eskimo rapist has is trying to get wet leather leggings off a woman who doesn't want to take them off. Have you ever tried to pull leather pants off someone who's trying to kick you in the nuts? It takes a lot of effort. And, in the process, you would lose your hard-on. In fact, at the North Pole your dick would shrivel up like a stack of dimes.

That's another thing I wonder. Does a rapist have a hard-on when he leaves the house in the morning? Or does it develop during the day while he's walking around checkin' out the gals? Just wondering.

THE EVENING NEWS

* Police in Maine announced today they have broken up a ring of amphetamine users. Six of the speed freaks were arrested on the spot. Another four got away by sprinting completely across Canada.

* It has been disclosed that several years ago when Mother Teresa won the Nobel Peace Prize, she returned the money, claiming it had germs on it.

* A man who was attempting to walk around the world drowned today on the first leg of his journey, which would have taken him from San Francisco to Honolulu.

* The owner of a Florida massage parlor has been arrested by police. "There weren't any serious violations," said the officers, "she just rubbed us the wrong way."

* Doctors treating a ninety-year-old pregnant woman claim that because of her advanced age she will have a grown-up.

* A Boston man who last year shot and killed all twelve members of a jury that convicted him of murder goes on trial again today. Courtroom insiders say jury selection is expected to take quite some time.

* Silent film star Mark Dunbar died today in Hollywood. He had no last words; however, he did wiggle his eyebrows and make several exaggerated gestures with his arms.

* A Cincinnati man has revealed that last month a local hospital, instead of giving him a vasectomy, castrated him. A hospital spokesman explained, "It all started as a joke. The doctors pre-

tended they were going to castrate him, but he got real snotty so they went ahead and did it to teach him a lesson." The patient, though upset, seemed philosophical. "The way I look at it, it's that much less to wash."

✳ A New Hampshire inventor has developed a machine he claims will grant him any wish. Reporters were greeted at his home by hundreds of naked women who said they had been blowing him for the past six months.

✳ A sixty-five-year-old fitness expert trotting backward from Winnipeg to Chile in an effort to promote backward trotting was killed today when she was hit by a truck head-on from the rear.

✳ And finally, on the lighter side, here's a human-interest story about man's best friend. It seems sixty-five-year-old James Driscoll was asleep in his downtown hotel room last week when he was awakened by the sound of a dog barking. When he awoke the room was filled with smoke, and he could not see to get out. The dog led him out of the room, down the hall, and into an elevator shaft, where he plunged eight stories to his death. It seems it wasn't his dog.

DANCE CALLED BECAUSE OF RAIN

When I think of the rain dance the American Indians used to do, I often wonder if they had to practice first. Wouldn't you want to have rain-dance practice just to go over things again? To make sure everyone was doing the correct steps in the correct order? Maybe there were some new guys; maybe the dance master had some new things he wanted to try out. There are all sorts of reasons why the Indians might want to play it safe and practice first.

My question is, if they did hold practice, and the rain didn't come immediately, how would they know they had done it right? If the dance is done correctly, shouldn't it rain? Or did the Indians figure the rain god knew it was only practice and was waiting for the real thing?

Then again, if it did rain right after practice, why not just cancel the dance and figure the next time you need rain all you have to do is practice?

These are the kinds of thoughts that made it necessary to separate me from the other kids in school.

THINGS THAT ARE PISSING ME OFF

Cigars

Haven't we had about enough of this cigar smoking shit? When are these fat, arrogant, overfed, white-collar business criminals going to extinguish their cigars and move along to their next abomination?

Soft, white, business pussies suckin' on a big brown dick. That's all it is, folks, a big, brown dick. You know, Freud used to say, "Sometimes a cigar is just a cigar." Yeah? Well, sometimes it's a big brown dick! With a fat, criminal-business asshole sucking on the wet end of it!

But, hey. The news is not all bad for me. Not all bad. Want to hear the good part? Cancer of the mouth. Good! Fuck 'em! Makes me happy; it's an attractive disease. So light up, suspender-man, and suck that smoke deep down into your empty suit. And blow it out your ass, you miserable cocksucker!

Angels

What is all this nonsense about angels? Do you realize three out of four Americans now believe in angels? What are they, fuckin' stupid? Has everybody lost their goddamn minds?

Angels, my ass! You know what I think it is? I think it's a massive, collective, chemical flashback from all the drugs—all the drugs!—smoked, swallowed, snorted, and shot up by all Americans from 1960 to 2000. Forty years of adulterated street drugs will get you some fuckin' angels, my friend!

Angels, shit. What about goblins? Doesn't anybody believe in goblins? And zombies. Where the fuck are all the zombies? That's the trouble with zombies, they're unreliable. I say if you're gonna buy that angel bullshit, you may as well go for the goblin-zombie package as well.

Bike Frauds

Here's another horrifying example of a declining American culture. The continued pussification of the male population, this time in the form of Harley Davidson theme restaurants. What is going on here?

Harley Davidson used to mean something; it stood for biker attitude; grimy outlaws and their sweaty mamas full of beer and crank, rollin' around on Harleys, lookin' for a good time. Destroying property, raping teenagers, and killing policemen. All very necessary activities.

But now . . . theme restaurants! And this soft shit obviously didn't come from hard-core bikers, it came from weekend motorcyclists. These fraudulent, two-day-a-week lames who have their bikes trucked into Sturgis, South Dakota, for the big rally and then ride around town like they just came off the road. Lawyers and dentists and pussy-boy software designers gettin' up on Harleys because they think it makes 'em cool. Well hey, Skeezix, you ain't cool, you're fuckin' chilly. And chilly ain't never been cool.

The House of Blues

I have a proposition: I think if white people are going to burn down black churches, then black people ought to burn down the House of Blues. What a disgrace that place is. The House of Blues. You know what they ought to call it? The House of Lame White Motherfuckers! Inauthentic, low-frequency, lame white motherfuckers.

Especially these male movie stars who think they're blues artists. You ever see these guys? Don't you just want to puke in your soup when one of these fat, overweight, out-of-shape, middle-aged, pasty-faced, baldy-headed movie stars with sunglasses jumps onstage and starts blowin' into a harmonica? It's a fuckin' sacrilege.

In the first place, white people got no business playing the blues ever. At all! Under any circumstances! What the fuck do white people have to be blue about? Banana Republic ran out of khakis? The espresso machine is jammed? Hootie and the Blowfish are breaking up?

Shit, white people ought to understand . . . their job is to *give* people the blues, not to get them. And certainly not to sing or play them! I'll tell you a little secret about the blues: it's not enough to know which notes to play, you have to know why they need to be played.

And another thing, I don't think white people should be trying to dance like blacks. Stop that! Stick to your faggoty polkas and waltzes, and that repulsive country line-dancing shit that you do, and be yourself. Be proud! Be white! Be lame! And get the fuck off the dance floor!

A Day in the Life of Henry VIII

Wake up
Fuck the queen
Take a shit
Kill the queen
Eat six chickens
Get married
Kill the new queen
Eat a cow
Take a shit
Start dating
Belch for an hour
Eat a sheep
Kill my date
Defy the pope
Eat a goat
Take a shit
Fuck a bishop
Get engaged
Kill my fiancée
Eat a pig
Marry a pig
Kill the pig
Eat the pope
Vomit
Go to sleep

FAMILIES WORTH LOATHING

Are you sick of this "royal family" shit? Who gives a fuck about these people? Who cares about the English in general? The uncivilized, murderous, backward English. Inbred savages hiding behind Shakespeare, pretending to be cultured. Don't be misled by the manners; if you want to know what lurks beneath the surface, take a look at the soccer crowds. That's the true British character. I'm Irish and I'm American, and we've had to kick these degenerate English motherfuckers out of both of our countries.

But most Americans are stupid; they like anything they're told they like. So when the duke and duchess of Wales or Windsor, or whatever, visit America, and people are asked if they like them, the simpletons say, "Yes, I like them a lot. They're sort of fun." If they asked me I would say, "Well, I'm Irish, and they've killed a lot of my people, so I wish they'd die in a fire. Maybe someone will blow up their limousine."

The English have systematically exploited and degraded this planet and its people for a thousand years. You know what I say? Let's honor the royal ladies: Queen Elizabeth, the Queen Mum, Margaret, Fergie, and all the rest. Let's give them the hot-lead douche. Get out the funnel, turn them upside-down, and give them the hot-lead douche. Right in their royal boxes. That's my message from the IRA to the English.

And I'm really glad the black, tan, and brown people of the world, fucked over by the English for so long, are coming home to Mother England to claim their property. England is now being invaded by the very people she plundered. They're flying, sailing, swimming, and rowing home to the seat of Empire, looking to the Crown: "Hey, mon! What about de food stamps?"

WHERE WAS I STANDING LAST TIME WE DID THIS?

When Britain returned Hong Kong to China there was a long, formal ceremony. The whole thing looked well-rehearsed, and I wondered how everyone knew exactly where to stand and what to do. After all, the event had never taken place before; how could there be a set of procedures? Do the British have a manual on returning colonies? If so, they won't be needing it much longer.

I notice the same thing is true when a pope or king dies.

The elaborate funerals involve at least thirty or forty groups of participants, each with different roles and different garb, and each of whom seems to know exactly where to walk, when to stop, and where to stand. And everyone knows all the songs and prayers by heart.

Can someone tell me when these people practice all this pageantry?

LIFE'S LITTLE MOMENTS

* Do you ever look at your watch and immediately forget the time, so you look again? And still it doesn't register, so you have to look a third time. And then someone asks you what time it is, and you actually have to look at your watch for the fourth time in three minutes? Don't you feel stupid?

* Do you ever find yourself standing in a room, and you can't remember why you went in there? And you think to yourself, "Maybe

if I go back where I was I'll see something that reminds me. Or maybe it would be quicker if I just stand here and hope it comes back to me." Usually as you're weighing those options, two words float across your mind: "Alzheimer's disease."

* Do you ever have to sneeze while you're taking a piss? It's frightening. Deep down you're afraid you'll release all sorts of bodily fluids into your pants. What people don't realize is that it's physically impossible to sneeze while pissing; your brain won't allow it. Because your brain knows you might blow your asshole out. And wind up having to repaint the entire apartment.

* Have you ever noticed how sometimes all day Wednesday you keep thinking it's Thursday? Then the next day when you're back to normal, you wonder, why don't you think it's Friday?

* Have you ever been sitting on a railroad train in the station, and another train is parked right next to you? And one of them begins moving, but you can't tell which one? And then it becomes obvious, and all the magic is gone? Wouldn't it be nice if we could spend our whole lives not knowing which train was moving? Actually, we do.

* Do you ever fall asleep in the late afternoon and wake up after dark, and for a moment you can't figure out what day it is? You actually find yourself thinking, Could this be yesterday?

* Did you ever tell someone they have a little bit of dirt on their face? They never rub the right spot, do they? They always assume the mirror image and rub the wrong side. Don't you just want to slap the bastard?

✳ Have you noticed that when your head is on the pillow, if you close one eye the pillow is in one position? But when you switch eyes the pillow seems to move? Sometimes I lie awake for hours doing that.

✳ Do you ever reach the top of a staircase and think there's one more step? So you take one of those big, awkward steps that doesn't accomplish anything? And then you have to do it a few more times, so people will think it's something you do all the time. "I do this all the time, folks. It's the third stage of syphilis."

The 10 Most Embarrassing Songs of All Time

1. *I Gotta Be Me*

2. *My Way*

3. *I Write the Songs*

4. *That's Life*

5. *Let Me Entertain You*

6. *Hey, Look Me Over*

7. *You're Gonna Hear From Me*

8. *Impossible Dream*

9. *I Will Survive*

10. *If They Could See Me Now*

SHORT TAKES

People often say, "That's a fine how-do-you-do," when deep in their hearts they know it's really only a fairly good how-do-you-do.

I've noticed there's such a thing as disposable douche. And I wonder Why would someone want to keep that stuff in the first place?

When I was young I used to read about the decline of Western civilization, and I decided it was something I would like to make a contribution to.

Have you noticed when you look in the top drawer of someone's desk there are always a few pennies in the pencil tray? I take them.

In a package of bacon, underneath all the neat horizontal strips there's always one oddly-folded piece that seems to have been thrown in at the last moment.

You rarely see one oat all by itself.

The best thing about living at the seashore is that you only have assholes on three sides of you. And if they come at you from the water, you can usually hear them splash.

Although it's untrue that rubbing a toad causes warts, it does give the toad a hard-on.

We will never be an advanced civilization as long as rain showers can delay the launching of a space rocket.

THE POPE WEARS LOAFERS

I never worry that all hell will break loose. My concern is that only part of hell will break loose and be much harder to detect.

What is all this dinner-and-a-movie shit? Why can't people just go somewhere and fuck for three or four hours?

In restaurants where they serve frog's legs, what do they do with the rest of the frog? Do they just throw it away? You never see "frog torsos" on the menu. Is there actually a garbage can full of frog bodies in the alley? I wouldn't want to be a homeless guy looking for an unfinished cheeseburger and open the lid on that.

I hope no one asks me to show them the ropes; I have no idea where they are. Maybe I could pull some strings and find out.

If you practice throwing the discus alone, you have to go get it yourself.

It's fun to go into the hospital room of a terminal patient and whisper to him, "Hang on. We're working on a miracle drug. It'll be ready in about five years."

I really don't care if we have a nuclear war as long as I can get some French fries.

I'm one of those people who hope Elvis Presley is really dead. Buddy Holly too. "The day the music died," shit. As far as I'm concerned, it was the day the music got better. All those guys did was steal and water down black music to make it safe and easy to digest for fearful white kids. Here's a toast to all the great black artists who got ripped off by no-talent white thieves.

One thing nice about being dead is that you immediately become eligible to appear on stamps and money.

Cat's thought: "I sure could do with a nice rat."

Oxen can be trained to genuflect and whistle softly in the moonlight.

Have you ever noticed the escalator handrail and the thing you're standing on don't move at the same speed?

You know what you rarely see? A ninety-three-year-old guy workin' on his résumé.

I don't mind government regulation, but requiring people to wear helmets during intercourse is a bit much.

Whom does a male ladybug dance with?

Did you ever notice that apparently the Lone Ranger and Tonto never got their laundry done?

I pray each night that someday on a single afternoon, several major news stories will break within a few hours of each other. I would love to see two 747s colliding above Times Square, the president and vice president getting assassinated, Iran and Israel having a nuclear exchange, the Dow Jones dropping 8,500 points, and California having an earthquake measuring 13.7. It would be fun watching the news channels try to cope with it all. And you know what would really be fun? Reading the newspapers for the following few weeks.

I know a transsexual guy whose only ambition is to eat, drink, and be Mary.

Not Much to Do Dept.: Someone has actually gone to the trouble of determining that Columbus, Ohio, has the best-dressed police force.

Here's how you get rid of counterfeit money: Put it in the collection plate at church.

I don't understand the problem some people have with paroling Charles Manson. I say set him free and let him get on with his work. I have a long list of celebrities I'd be glad to share with him.

When people say "clean as a whistle," they forget that a whistle is full of spit.

ORGAN DONOR PROGRAMS

I'm not too enthusiastic about this organ donor idea. What bothers me most is that it's run by the Motor Vehicles Bureau. I figure if I have to wait in line that long for a kidney, fuck it. I'll do without.

They send you a little card you're supposed to carry in your wallet next to your driver's license. You're supposed to list the organs you're willing to donate in case you die. Are these people crazy? Do you honestly believe that if a paramedic finds that card on you after an accident he's gonna be trying to save your life? No way! He's lookin' for parts.

"Look, Sid! Here's that lower intestine we've been hoping for. Never mind the CPR, this man's a donor!"

Fuck that. If these people want something of mine, they can have my appendix. That's it. That's all I'm giving. Put it in the cooler and get the fuck outta here.

Plugging Along

And don't go pulling any plugs on me, either. That's another bunch of macho bullshit floating around. People talkin' about, "Aw, just pull the plug on me. If I'm comatose? Lyin' there like a vegetable? Just go ahead and pull the plug."

And I say, FUCK YOU! LEAVE MY PLUG ALONE!! Get an extension cord for my plug! I want everything you got: tubes, cords, plugs, probes, electrodes, IVs. You find I got an orifice that's not bein' used, stick a fuckin' tube in it. Vegetable, shit! I don't care if I look like an artichoke. Save my ass!

If you ever find out I'm comatose just remember there are three things I gotta have: ice cream, morphine, and TV. Give me that ice cream about every two hours; give me that morphine about, oh, every ten minutes; and turn on the fuckin' TV!! I wanna watch *Survivor!*

And don't be comin' to visit me, either. I got no time for live people. I'm brain-dead, here. Ain't you people got no respect for the brain-dead? Hey, you gotta be brain-dead to watch *Survivor!* in the first place; you might as well watch it when you're clinically brain-dead.

Now, one more thought concerning this comatose stuff. This might come in handy someday. If you know a homosexual who is co-matose, remember, you can always comfort his family by saying, "Look at it this way, folks. He was a fruit, now he's a vegetable. At least he's still in the produce section."

ON THE BEACH: THE MOVIE

It is said that just before you die your life flashes before your eyes; especially if it's a sudden death. It's like a little personal movie of your own. But it doesn't make sense to me. Mathematically, how would it work?

Let's say you're swimming at the beach, you get caught in a rip-tide, and it pulls you out to sea. You panic and begin swallowing water. Since you're about to die, the flashback movie begins to roll.

It seems to me that if it's really a flashback of your entire life, you'd have to watch the whole thing, and that would include the ending. Which means seeing yourself arrive at the beach, walk into the surf, start to drown, and have the movie start all over again. Therefore you'd have to watch it a second time, which would include arriving at the beach, walking into the surf, and . . . you get what I mean? Thanks to the flashback, you can never die. The movie runs forever.

"I COULDN'T COMMIT SUICIDE IF MY LIFE DEPENDED ON IT"

So Little Time

Whenever I hear that someone has committed suicide I wonder one thing. Not Why did he do it? or What was he thinking? I wonder, How did he find the time? Who has time to be running around committing suicide these days? Aren't you busy? Don't you have things to do? I do. Suicide would be way down on my list. It would come much later, for example, than setting my neighbor's house on fire. Believe me, I would have to work suicide into an already very crowded schedule. I'd probably try a little self-mutilation at first, just to get started. See if I like the general concept.

When you think about it, the planning alone would create all sorts of tasks. First, you'd have to choose a method. That's big. And that might take a while; there are so many good ways to go.

"Let's see. How about firing a gun in my mouth? Naaah! Jesus, that would hurt. And suppose I lived? My head would have a big hole in the top. Fuck that. Maybe I should just hang myself. No, too weird. I don't want people to think I'm weird. Just sad. Really, really sad. I guess I could put my head in the oven and turn on the gas. Shit, it's an electric oven. What am I gonna do? I'm afraid of heights, I have trouble swallowing pills, and I can't stand the sight of blood. God, this is depressing. I know! I'll throw myself in front of a subway train. No, I live in Cheyenne. Damn! Maybe I'll just eat some infected dog shit."

Dear Survivor

You also have to decide whether or not to leave a note. You might just think, Fuck 'em. Let 'em figure it out for themselves. And I really think not leaving a note is a nice touch, especially if you're a perky, optimistic, happily married person and recently got a big promotion. Let 'em figure it out for themselves.

But, remember, if you do leave a note you'll have to come up with a version you're satisfied with. You have to get it right.

"Let's see, 'To whom it may concern.' No, too impersonal. 'Dear Myra.' No, that leaves out the kids. I've got it! 'Hi, everybody. Guess what?' "

Or you may want to go for maximum survivor-guilt: "To all of you who drove me to this, you know who you are. I hope you're satisfied, now that I've destroyed myself."

How about simply saying, "Hi. Hope this note finds you healthy and happy. Not me. Healthy, not happy. In fact, wait'll you read the rest of this note."

Suppose you're a writer? Seems to me, a writer would get so involved revising and polishing the note that he'd never get around to the suicide. He would cheer up just by writing a really good note. Then he'd turn it into a book proposal.

Another problem for suicide people is the timing. "Okay, Tuesday's out, gotta take Timmie to the circus; Wednesday's my colon cleansing; the play-offs start on Friday; my folks'll be here for the weekend. Hmmm! The weekend . . ."

I feel sorry for these suicide people. There are so many things to think about. Don't get me wrong, I'm still glad they do it; I find it highly entertaining. It certainly qualifies as drama: an irreversible act that puts a permanent end to your consciousness. Talk about a big decision; you'd better be thinking clearly. You gotta be at your best for suicide.

Must-Die TV

I just love the whole idea. I could really appreciate an all-suicide channel. Boy, you talk about reality programming: One person after another, destroying themselves permanently in front of the entire nation. And never mind that V-chip shit, let the kids watch. Teach 'em they have options in life. I would show every method imaginable. And when there's a lull in the action, I'd run films of World War II kamikaze raids and Arab suicide bombers.

I think you could get big ratings with suicide. Especially if you had unusual methods. I'll bet anything you could get 200 people in this country to hold hands and jump into the Grand Canyon. Sick people, old people, the chronically depressed. And to get young folks involved, instead of calling it suicide, you bill it as "extreme living." Put it on TV and give some of the profits to the surviving relatives.

CEO Is D.O.A.

But I digress. You know what I really like about suicide? The reasons some people give. Like those Japanese businessmen who bankrupt their companies through bad management and decide to end it all. Imagine a guy in a three-piece gray suit and red tie, opening his briefcase, taking out a fourteen-inch fish knife, and slashing his stomach open eighteen inches from side to side. Wow! If that tie wasn't red before it sure is now. By the way, this would be a really good idea for those Firestone and Ford executives.

No Coin Return

I love suicide. You know what they ought to have in amusement arcades? Coin-operated suicide machines. Simple idea. You sit down at a steel table and deposit 50 cents. There's a thirty-second delay as you lean forward, place your head on the table, and put your arms behind your back. Before long, you hear, "Five, four, three, two, one." Then a large cast-iron hammer comes slamming down with 2,000 pounds of force and smashes your head to bits. And it keeps on smashing for about twenty minutes, to give you your money's worth. Lets you rest in pieces.

EUPHEMISTIC BULLSHIT

I don't like euphemistic language, words that shade the truth. American English is packed with euphemism, because Americans have trouble dealing with reality, and in order to shield themselves from it they use soft language. And somehow it gets worse with every generation.

Here's an example. There's a condition in combat that occurs when a soldier is completely stressed out and is on the verge of nervous collapse. In World War I it was called "shell shock." Simple, honest, direct language. Two syllables. Shell shock. It almost sounds like the guns themselves. That was more than eighty years ago.

Then a generation passed, and in World War II the same combat condition was called "battle fatigue." Four syllables now; takes a little longer to say. Doesn't seem to hurt as much. "Fatigue" is a nicer word than "shock." Shell shock! Battle fatigue.

By the early 1950s, the Korean War had come along, and the very same condition was being called "operational exhaustion." The phrase was up to eight syllables now, and any last traces of humanity had been completely squeezed out of it. It was absolutely sterile: operational exhaustion. Like something that might happen to your car.

Then, barely fifteen years later, we got into Vietnam, and, thanks to the deceptions surrounding that war, it's no surprise that the very same condition was referred to as "post-traumatic stress disorder." Still eight syllables, but we've added a hyphen, and the pain is completely buried under jargon: post-traumatic stress disorder. I'll bet if they had still been calling it "shell shock," some of those Vietnam veterans might have received the attention they needed.

But it didn't happen, and one of the reasons is that soft language; the language that takes the life out of life. And somehow it keeps getting worse.

Here are some more examples. At some point in my life, the following changes occurred:

toilet paper = bathroom tissue

sneakers = running shoes

false teeth = dental appliances

medicine = medication

information = directory assistance

the dump = the landfill

motels = motor lodges

house trailers = mobile homes

used cars = previously owned vehicles

room service = guest room dining

riot = civil disorder

strike = job action

zoo = wildlife park

jungle = rain forest

swamp = wetlands

glasses = presciption eyewear

garage = parking structure

drug addiction = substance abuse

soap opera = daytime drama

gambling joint = gaming resort

prostitute = sex worker

theater = performing arts center

wife beating = domestic violence

constipation = occasional irregularity

Health

When I was a little boy, if I got sick I went to a doctor, who sent me to a hospital to be treated by other doctors. Now I go to a "family practitioner," who belongs to a "health maintenance organization," which sends me to a "wellness center" to be treated by "health-care delivery professionals."

Poverty

Poor people used to live in slums. Now "the economically disadvantaged" occupy "substandard housing" in the "inner cities." And a lot of them are broke. They don't have "negative cash flow." They're broke! Because many of them were fired. In other words, management wanted to "curtail redundancies in the human resources area," and so, many workers are no longer "viable members of the workforce." Smug, greedy, well-fed white people have invented a language to conceal their sins. It's as simple as that.

Government

The CIA doesn't kill anybody, they "neutralize" people. Or they "depopulate" an area. The government doesn't lie, it engages in "disinformation." The Pentagon actually measures nuclear radiation in something called "sunshine units." Israeli murderers are called "commandos," Arab commandos are called "terrorists." The contra killers were known as "freedom fighters." Well, if crime fighters fight crime and firefighters fight fire, what do freedom fighters fight?

Physical Disorders

And some of this softened language is just silly and embarrassing. On the airlines they say they're going to preboard "passengers in need of special assistance." Cripples. Simple, honest, direct language. There's no shame attached to the word "cripple." No shame. It's a word used in Bible translations: "Jesus healed the cripples." It doesn't take six words to describe that condition.

But we don't have cripples anymore; instead we have the "physically challenged." Is that a grotesque enough evasion for you? How about "differently abled?" I've actually heard cripples referred to as differently abled. You can't even call them handicapped anymore. They say, "We're not handicapped, we're handi-capable." These poor suckers have been bullshitted by the system into believing that if you change the name of the condition, somehow you'll change the condition. Well, it doesn't happen that way.

I'm sure you've noticed we have no deaf people in this country. "Hearing impaired." And no one's blind. "Partially sighted" or "visually impaired." And thank God we no longer have stupid children. Today's kids all have "learning disabilities." Or they're "minimally exceptional." How would you like to be told that about your child? Actually, it sounds faintly positive.

"He's minimally exceptional."

"Oh, thank God for that, I guess."

Best of all, psychologists now call ugly people "those with severe appearance deficits." Things are so bad that any day I expect to hear a rape victim referred to as an unwilling sperm recipient.

Gettin' Old

Of course, it's been obvious for some time that there are no old people in this country. They all died, and what we have are "senior citizens." How's that for a lifeless, typically American, twentieth-century phrase? There's no pulse in a "senior citizen."

But that's a term I've come to accept. That's what old people are going be called. But the phrase I will continue to resist is when they describe an old person as being "ninety years young." Imagine how sad the fear of aging that is revealed in that phrase. To be unable even to use the word "old"; to have to use its antonym.

And I understand the fear of aging is natural; it's universal, isn't it? No one wants to get old, no one wants to die. But we do. We die. And we don't like that, so we bullshit ourselves.

I started bullshitting myself when I reached my forties. I'd look in the mirror, and say, "Well, I guess I'm getting . . . 'older!' " Older sounds better than old, doesn't it? Sounds like it might even last a little longer. Bullshit. I'm getting old. And it's okay. But the Baby Boomers can't handle that, and remember, the boomers invented most of this soft language. So now they've come up with a new life phase: "pre-elderly." How sad. How relentlessly sad.

Gettin' Dead

But it's all right, folks, because thanks to our fear of death, no one has to die; they can all just pass away. Or expire, like a magazine subscription. If it happens in the hospital, it will be called a terminal episode. The insurance company will refer to it as negative patient-care outcome. And if it's the result of malpractice, they'll say it was a therapeutic misadventure.

To be honest, some of this language makes me want to vomit. Well, perhaps "vomit" is too strong a word. It makes me want to engage in an involuntary, personal protein spill.

BEER AND POT

When I was young, most kids in my neighborhood drank beer before they discovered pot. Everybody drank first. Saturday night we drank beer and puked on our shoes. It was an Irish neighborhood. Drink and puke, that was it. A great American tradition. It still goes on today.

Then in 1950, when I was thirteen, we heard about pot. We discovered that on pot you didn't stagger, you didn't puke on your shoes, and your breath didn't smell. Which was important. Because, as a kid, when you came home from drinking there were two breath smells that could give you away: alcohol and puke.

So, we found that when you smoked pot, you could withstand your mother's closest scrutiny. Because, let's face it, you had come home drunk so often wearing someone else's clothing that your mother was now openly asking to smell your breath.

"Come here, mister! Let me smell the breath. Ahhh! No booze or puke. That's a good boy. What's that under your arm?"

"Two boxes of Oreos."

"That's a good boy."

"Good night, Ma."

Cool.

HIGH ON THE PLANE

Airlines disappoint me. Why don't they have a flight attendant whose job it is to hand out drugs? They're certainly aggressive enough when it comes to alcohol. Even before the meal begins they're in the aisles: "Champagne, red wine, white wine?" Can't they spare one person to wander around muttering, "Coke? Smoke? Chance to get high. Crank? Acid? Smack? You're high in the plane, now get high *on* the plane!"

For me, on a long flight it used to be that gettin' high was half the fun. Hell, even a short flight. Lockin' myself in the bathroom, firin' up a joint. That's what flyin' was all about. Now you can't smoke anything at all, not even a good old-fashioned ready-roll. They have smoke detectors. Jesus! The people in this country have really become a pack of fearful, ignorant sheep. Everybody's a God-fearing, law-abiding asshole now. Fair warning, my friend: if you're gonna smoke a joint on the airplane these days, you better be an old pro.

In the old days I always did my pot-smoking in the forward lavatory, because I fantasized that the mirror was two-way, and the crew could see me. I can't help it, I just like an audience. But I knew my manners; I always offered the crew a hit or two. I'd make little gestures with the joint toward the mirror. "C'mon, boys, lighten up. Life isn't all azimuth indicators." Never any takers; real straight folks up there.

Now, I'm sure all of you high-minded, non-chance-takers out there are thinkin', "What about the smell? Doesn't the bathroom fill up with pot smoke?" Well, folks, this is where a background in physics comes in handy. Follow me closely on this.

Before the airlines introduced those fancy new toilets, the ones that tear your genitals off when they flush, the old toilets, in order to control odors, had a slow, steady stream of air that flowed from the lavatory itself down into the bowl. And you could increase the speed of that airflow by simply sitting on the toilet, thereby reducing the size of the air passage down to that little wedge-shaped space between your thighs. Narrower channel, stronger flow. And your cheeks acted as a gasket, sealing off the rest of the opening.

Then, if you carefully pointed a lit cigarette down into the toilet between your thighs, all the smoke got sucked away into that mysterious, blue-chemical void. No smoke, no smell, no problem. By the way, I cannot overemphasize the importance of the word *carefully* in the above sentence.

Of course, not all planes had equally strong airflow, so a system test was always in order. A good physicist never proceeds without checking conditions. In this case, we use a common match. A lit match, quickly extinguished, produces a small, visible wisp of smoke. If the match is held deep in the bowl, one can observe whether that smoke is sucked straight downward or rises gently back into the lav. In the former case all systems are "go," in the latter case the No Smoking sign is wisely observed. Unless, of course, we decide to go to Plan B. One must always have a backup.

And so, we turn our attention to the sink. The sink is a magnificent device: it fills with water, holds it awhile, and then, when the drain is released, it empties. And on an airplane, when it empties it is helped along by what? Why, it's helped along by our old friend, Mr. Air Pressure! And, whaddaya know, just by pressing down on the drain-release plunger we can produce an even stronger flow of air than we can with the toilet, because the sink drain is so much smaller. A quick test with a lit match confirms this.

But remember, the drain-release lever is spring-loaded, and therefore if the airflow is to remain constant, the plunger must remain depressed and open during the entire period the joint is lit. And that means we have to prop the drain cap open by wedging some object underneath it. A matchbook cover, or perhaps one of those little bars of soap the airlines used to leave near the sink. Isn't science fun?

All right, gang, we're almost ready to light up and get wasted, but there is still one further consideration. If you're going to smoke a joint while seated on the toilet (as opposed to standing up, leaning down into the sink), at some point, you have to decide whether or not you should pretend to be taking a shit. In other words, whether or not to pull your pants down.

If you really have to take a shit at the time, that's great; you're all set. But if you don't, you have a decision to make. Because, although ethically there is nothing wrong with taking a fake shit, in a practical sense if the crew thinks you've been in there too long, and they decide to break down the door, you want to be sure that when they arrive you appear to be taking a genuine shit. Don't forget, they're going to check. And nobody wants to be arrested for shitting with his pants on, am I right? Although personally I can tell you I don't care what the charge is as long as I get rid of the joint. Besides, shitting with your pants on is only a misdemeanor. And in my case it would be a first offense.

Which brings us back to my own personal airline-bathroom experience. One problem I always had was that after I got high I would wind up staying in the bathroom way too long. Pot brought out the superorganizer in me, so once I'd had a few good, deep hits and was securely locked in, I tended to go to work.

First thing I did was open up all those little compartments un-der the sink and rearrange the supplies stored in there. I'd restack all the sanitary napkins according to strength: regular, super, jumbo, teeny-bopper. I'd remove the outer wrappers from the spare toilet pa-per, making it readily available in the event some nasty bacterium found its way into the first-class entrees. Then I'd refill the paper towel dispenser, being careful to pack it so tightly that the towels would not come out without shredding. And—again, the old days— I'd make sure there were plenty of those little bars of soap lying out for people to steal. In the occasional instance when cologne, after-shave, and other amenities were made available, I would be sure to take them home for further quality-control testing. Ford is not the only place where quality is job one.

Then, my chores done, I would relax somewhat and reflect on the environment around me. I'd become fascinated by the little slot they had for used razor blades, and I wondered whether or not the blades actually dropped out of the airplane and fell on people's houses, or if they just rusted and rotted somewhere behind the wall. I'd read the various signs posted in three languages and try to translate precisely the corresponding words in each language. Then, finally, a long, lingering look in the mirror, usually resulting in the discovery of some hideous facial flaw, previously undetected.

And then, suddenly, the little lighted sign would flash on telling me to Return to Cabin! Return to Cabin! Return to Cabin!

I'd think, Oh shit, trouble in the cabin. They need me. I should never have left them alone. I'd better see what's up. And then on my way out, I'd spot one last sign: Please Leave Lavatory Clean for the Next Passenger. Well, that's all I needed to see. And because I'm really into detail now—and even though I didn't make a mess—I'm experi-encing "felon's guilt." And I decide to clean up for the next person.

I rinse and dry and thoroughly polish the entire sink area, scouring all the burst-pimple residue off the mirror, and I even wash off the dried, gray dirt bubbles left on the soap by the previous person. Now I'm gettin' into it! Pretty soon I find myself washing the walls and ceiling, throwing open the door, and yelling, "You people got some Spic and Span and a hard-bristle brush out there? I think I can get these blue stains off the toilet!"

And suddenly I realize my fantasy world has collapsed; the real world is watching. Adjusting quickly, and relying on my identity as a comedian, I chuckle weakly and say, "You gotta clean up for the next person."

Then, as the fat woman waiting to take a shit passes me on her way into the john, I hiss, "Don't fuck it up, lady. I worked my ass off in there." And back to my seat I go, secure in the knowledge that, once again, thanks to my highly developed work ethic, along with some great Humboldt weed, I've managed to make the skies a little friendlier.

SHORT TAKES

You know one of the biggest rip-offs in the world? Flowers. They grow free all over the world, and yet we pay for them. And then they die. That seems strange. Flowers are one of the few things we buy, bring home, watch die, and we don't ask for our money back. Normally, we'd be screaming at a merchant over something like that: "Hey, what kind of shit is this? Gimme my money back! The fuckin' things keeled over right on the piano!"

The caterpillar does all the work, but the butterfly gets all the publicity.

Tits always look better in a pink sweater.

You know what you don't see enough of on television? A good parachute accident. It's kinda fun.

Ask your dry cleaner if he can remove the stains from one pair of pants and put them in another. He should be able to do that for the same amount of money. While you're in there, ask if he can remove semen from a wedding veil. That's the test of a really good dry cleaner.

To me, fast food is when a cheetah eats an antelope.

Two men whose names you see a lot on air-conditioner dials: Norm and Max.

Have you ever been kissing someone, and one of you has a snot that's whistling? It takes your mind off the sex, because it requires a three-step solution. First of all, you have to figure out whose nose it's in. Then you have to determine which nostril. Finally, someone has to dig in there and, if not remove it completely, at least push it to one side so it doesn't whistle anymore. By the way, during all this activity the man usually loses his hard-on.

A crumb is a great thing: If you break a crumb in half you don't get two half-crumbs, you get two crumbs. Doesn't that violate some law of physics?

I think I am, therefore, I am. I think.

Have you ever noticed that when you're torturing a person, after a while you get real tired and you don't know what to do to him next? Then you think of something, and you sort of get your energy back?

Any man with a small moustache wearing a bow tie and a loud vest is an asshole.

A cat will blink when struck with a hammer.

Reception lines would be a lot more interesting if instead of shaking hands, people greeted each other with a kick in the groin.

The reason the mainstream is thought of as a stream is because of its shallowness.

Actual bumper sticker: HORN BROKE—WATCH FOR FINGER.

Fun at the ballpark: Y'ever notice a lot of guys bring a glove to the game to catch a foul ball? Never mind that, bring a bat! When a foul ball comes flying toward you, BAM! Hit it back to the players. Everyone will sense you're a fun fan. They'll be glad they came to the ballpark on straitjacket night.

I read somewhere that for the average person fourteen farts a day are considered normal. Based on these figures, and judging from my own output, I have to assume there are millions of people who never fart at all.

I don't have a fear of heights. I do, however, have a fear of *falling* from heights.

Isn't it a good feeling when you read the tabloids and realize that a lot of famous people are just as fucked up as you are?

The justice system should have a penalty whereby they send you to prison, and for ten years the guards take turns doing that Three Stooges, jabbing-two-fingers-in-your-eyes thing. I think that would straighten a lot of guys out.

.backwards sentences say to used I !shit Oh !again go I There

I noticed in the newspaper that track and field has an event called the women's pole vault. It makes me wonder: With all the options available to her in this age, how does a young woman get interested in pole-vaulting? It seems like a bizarre choice. By the way, I hope you noticed I completely ignored the obvious opportunity for a cheap phallic joke.

If I ever lose my mind I hope some honest person will find it and take it to Lost and Found.

In some hotels they give you a little sewing kit. You know what I do? I sew the towels together. One time I sewed a button on a lampshade. I like to leave a mark.

What's wrong with America: There are schools in Fairfax County, Virginia, where kids are not allowed to win soccer games. Whenever a team gets two goals ahead they have to give up one player. Pathetic.

The Asian country known as Mongolia used to be called Outer Mongolia. And just below the Outer Mongolian border with China there was an autonomous region called Inner Mongolia. And since each of them had its own inner and outer regions, that means that at one time there existed, fairly close to one another, an "outer Inner Mongolia" and an "inner Outer Mongolia." I like that sort of thing. I like picturing the road signs and all the people taking wrong turns.

When someone with an artificial heart dies, I think they should take out the heart, hook it up to an artificial body, and let it go at that.

I never bite my nails; I consider it a health risk. Instead, I twist my nails off with pliers and burn away any excess tissue with a cigarette lighter.

SPORTS SHOULD BE FIXED: FIRST HALF

Everyone knows by now, sports is big business. But the major sports have grown boring and predictable, and the public has become jaded. So I'm suggesting a few changes that would add excitement to the games and increase their entertainment value.

Take Me Out to the Hospital

Baseball has one major problem: not enough serious injuries. A lot of baseball's so-called injuries are just "a strained this" or "a sore whatchamacallit." In today's culture that's not good enough. Fans are crying out for someone to be hurt really badly.

So, to raise the injury level, what I would do is place thirty to forty land mines in the outfield; the kind of mines that spray thousands of tiny nails when they explode. Not only would this add excitement, it would also provide a refreshing element of surprise: "There's a high, lazy fly ball to right field. O'Neill drifts over, pats his glove . . ." BOOOOOOM! "Holy fuckin' shit! Oh, good Lord! Oh, precious, precious Lord!"

Baseball is also accused of being too slow. Here's something that would not only speed up the game but also provide a welcome opportunity for serious injuries. Like most good ideas, it's uncomplicated: if the pitcher hits the batter with the ball, the batter is out. That's it. A simple idea, but it could make quite a difference.

And maybe if the ball hits the batter in the head it could be a double play. I don't know, I'm not an expert on rules. But it's certainly worth a try. And just think: a good "control pitcher" could have a perfect game just by hitting twenty-seven guys in a row. In fact, if you had two quality pitchers out there, the fans could be out of that ballpark in half an hour, on their way home to watch football on TV. Where they could see some *serious* goddamn injuries.

Gettin' My Kicks

Now, football. For many of you fans, football is already a perfect game. Its particular combination of speed, strategy, and brute force seems just right for the American psyche. But even a well-thought-out game like football can use a little help from a fun-loving guy like me.

I would start by improving the coin toss, by making it a full-contact event. While the coin is in the air, the team captains should be allowed to kick the officials. It would get things going on a positive note. Remember, this is a sport that owes its origin to the practice of English soldiers playfully kicking around the head of a Dane during the lulls in combat.

Now, to the game itself. I think football should limit itself to only one rule: Each down begins in an orderly manner. That's it. After that, the players should be allowed to do whatever they want. If there's a fight, you move it off to one side of the field. Let it run its course; no restrictions. If several 300-pound linemen are crippling a placekicker, fine. Let them continue. We shouldn't be trying to suppress the natural exuberance of athletes. Keep in mind these men are physical freaks, full of drugs and anger, and they're here to entertain us. They enjoy being injured; let them go about their business.

So much for upgrading the violence. Here's my suggestion for adding excitement. Currently, each team is allowed forty-five players on the squad, but most of them stand around watching the game from the sidelines. If I were in charge, this would not be happening. Instead, I would have all ninety men out on the field at all times. Offense, defense, special teams. Everyone. What football really needs is ninety steroid monstrosities geeked on amphetamines racing around the field trying to hurt one another.

Here's another way to spice up the game: leave the injured players on the field. Let them lie there. These men are supposed to be tough, you can't coddle them just because they break something. Let the other guys play around them. If they get stepped on, tough titty. These macho pinheads are always talking about how it's "a big war goin' on out there." Fine. Let the Red Cross come around and pick them up.

And regarding this taunting behavior that so many people find offensive, I don't see the problem. In fact, I don't think taunting goes nearly far enough. In my opinion—and I'm certainly no professional athlete—after a good hard tackle the defensive player should be allowed to pull down his pants and masturbate on the man he tackled. It seems like a simple thing, but it would change the whole tempo of the game. And if he can't ejaculate because 60,000 people are watching, you hit him with a 15-yard penalty for delay of game.

I end my suggestions for improving football by taking a look at one of those game-end rituals: the pouring of Gatorade on the winning coach. To my mind, this is far too fruity for football. It's barely appropriate for a sixth-grade dodgeball team. What ought to happen is the winning team should be allowed to come across the field and spike the losing coach. Just spike him. Four linebackers turn him upsidedown and pile-drive him headfirst into the ground. Give him an incentive to work a little harder on the next week's game plan.

CAPITAL PUNISHMENT

Many people in this country want to expand the death penalty to include drug dealers. This is really stupid. Drug dealers aren't afraid to die. They're already killin' each other by the hundreds every day. Drive-bys, turf wars, gang killings. They're not afraid to die. The death penalty means very little unless you use it on people who are afraid to die. Like the bankers who launder the drug money. Forget dealers. If you want to slow down the drug traffic, you have to start executing some of these white, middle-class Republican bankers. And I don't mean soft American executions like lethal injection. I'm talkin' about crucifixion, folks. I say bring back crucifixion! A form of capital punishment the Christians and Jews of America can really appreciate.

And I'd take it a step further: I'd crucify these people upside-down. Like St. Peter. Feet up, head down. And naked! I'd have naked, upside-down crucifixions once a week on TV, at halftime of the Monday Night Football games. The Monday Night Crucifixions! Shit, you'd have people tunin' in who don't even care about football. Wouldn't you like to hear Dennis Miller explain why the nails have to go in at a specific angle?

And I'll guarantee you one thing: you start nailin' one white banker per week to a big wooden cross on national television, and you're gonna see that drug traffic begin to slow down mighty fuckin' quick. Why you won't even be able to buy drugs in schools and prisons anymore.

Personally, I don't care about capital punishment one way or another, because I know it doesn't do anything. It doesn't really do anything, except satisfy the biblical need for revenge. You know, if you read the Bible, you see it's filled with violence, retribution, and revenge.

So capital punishment is really kind of a religious ritual. A purification rite. It's a modern sacrament.

And as long as that's true, I say let's liven it up. Let's add a little show business. I believe if you make capital punishment a little more entertaining, and market it correctly, you can raise enough money to save Social Security.

And remember, the polls show the American people want capital punishment, and they want Social Security. And I think even in a fake democracy people ought to get what they want once in a while. If for no other reason than to feed the illusion that they're really in charge. Let's use capital punishment the same way we use sports and shopping in this country: to take people's minds off how badly they're bein' fucked by the upper 1 percent.

Now, unfortunately the football season only lasts about six months. What we really need is capital punishment year-round. Put it on TV every night with sponsors. Ya gotta have sponsors. I'm sure as long as we're killing people, Dow Chemical and Marlboro cigarettes will be proud to participate. Save Social Security.

And not only do I recommend crucifixions, I'm also in favor of bringing back beheadings. Wouldn't that be great? Beheadings on TV, complete with slow-motion and instant replay. And maybe you could let the heads roll down a little hill and fall into one of five numbered holes. Let the folks at home gamble on which hole the head is gonna fall into. Interactive television snuff-gambling! Give the people what they want.

And you do it in a stadium, so the rabble can gamble on it too. Raise a little more money. And, if you want to extend the violence a little longer—to sell a few extra commercials—instead of using an ax, you do the beheadings with a handsaw. And don't bother getting queasy at this point, folks, the blood's already on your hands; all we're talking about now is a matter of degree. You want something a little more delicate? We could do the beheadings with an olive fork. That would be good. And the nice part is, it would take a real long time.

There are a lot of good things you could do with capital punishment. When's the last time we burned someone at the stake? It's been too long! Here's another form of state killing that comes from a rich religious tradition: burning people at the stake. Put it on TV on Sunday mornings; the Sunday-morning, evangelical, send-us-an-offering, praise Jesus, human bonfire. You don't think that would get big ratings? In this sick fuckin' country? Shit, you'd have people skippin' church to watch this stuff. And then you take the money from the prayer offerings and use it to save Social Security.

And whatever happened to boiling people in oil? Remember that? Let's bring it back. On TV. First you get the oil goin' good with a nice high rolling boil. And then slowly, at the end of a rope, you lower the prisoner, headfirst, into the boiling oil. Boy, you talk about fun shit! And to encourage citizen participation, you let the rabble in the stadium control the speed of the rope. Good, clean, wholesome family entertainment. The kids'll love it. No V-chip to spoil the fun. And all the while they're enjoying themselves, we're teachin' them a nice Christian moral lesson. Boiling people in oil.

And maybe, instead of boiling all these guys, every now and then you could French-fry a couple of 'em. French-fried felons! Or dip a guy in egg batter, just for a goof. Kind of a tempura thing. Jeffrey Dahmer never thought of that, did he? Jeffrey Dahmer, eat your heart out! Which is an interesting thought in and of itself.

All right, enough nostalgia. How about some modern forms of capital punishment? How about throwin' a guy off the roof of the World Trade Center, and whoever he lands on wins the Publishers Clearinghouse?

Or perhaps something more sophisticated. You dip a guy in brown gravy and lock him in a small room with a wolverine who's high on angel dust. That's one guy who's not gonna be fuckin' with the kids at the bus stop.

Here's a good one. Something really nice. You take a high-speed catapult, and you shoot a guy straight into a brick wall. Trouble is, it would be over too quickly. No good for TV. You'd have to do a whole bunch of guys right in a row. Rapid-fire capital punishment. Fifteen catapults! While you're shootin' off one, you're loadin' up the others. Of course, every now and then you'd have to stop everything to clean off the wall. Cleanliness! Right next to godliness.

Finally, high-tech! I sense you're waitin' for some high-tech. Here you go. You take a highly miniaturized tactical nuclear weapon, and you stick it straight up a guy's ass and set it off. A thermonuclear suppository. Preparation H-Bomb. Boy, you talk about fallout! Or, a variation: You put a bomb inside that little hole on the end of a guy's dick. A bomb in a dick! And when it goes off, the guy wouldn't know whether he was comin' or goin'! I got a lotta good ideas. Save Social Security.

FARM SYSTEM: THUGS, PERVS, NUTS, AND DRUNKS

Here's another one of my really good ideas. I'm going to save us a whole lot of money on prisons, but at the same time I'm going to remove from society many of our more annoying citizens. Four groups are goin' away—permanently!

First group: Violent criminals. Here's what you do: You take the entire state of Kansas and you move everybody out. You give the people a couple of hundred dollars apiece for their inconvenience, but you get them out. Next you put a 100-foot-high electric fence around the entire state, and Kansas becomes a permanent prison farm for violent criminals. No police, no parole, no supplies; the only thing you give them is lethal weapons and live ammunition. So they can communicate in a meaningful manner.

Then you put the whole thing on cable TV. The Violence Network. VNN. And for a corporate sponsor, you get one of those companies that loves to smear its logo-feces all over the landscape. Budweiser will jump at this in half a minute.

Second group: Sex criminals. Completely incurable; you have to lock them up. Oh, I suppose you could outlaw religion and these sex crimes would disappear in a generation or two, but we don't have time for rational solutions. It's much easier to fence off another rectangular state. This time, Wyoming.

But this is only for true sex offenders. We're not going to harass consenting adults who dress up in leather Boy Scout uniforms and smash each other in the head with ball-peen hammers as they take turns blowing their cats. There's nothing wrong with that; it's a victimless hobby. And think of how happy the cat must be. No, we're only going to lock up rapists and molesters; those hopeless romantics who are so full of love they can't help gettin' a little of it on you. Usually on your leg.

You take all these heavy-breathing fun-seekers, and you stick them in Wyoming. And you let them suck, fuck, and fondle. You let them blow, chew, sniff, lick, whip, gobble, and cornhole one other . . . until their testicles are whistlin' "O Come All Ye Faithful." Then you turn on the cameras, and you've got . . . the Semen Channel! And don't forget our corporate sponsor. We're going to let Budweiser put little logo patches on the rapists' pants: "This pud's for you!"

Next group: Drug addicts and alcoholics. Not all of them, don't get nervous. Just the ones who are making life difficult for at least one other person. And we're not gonna bother first offenders; people deserve a chance to clean up. So, everyone will get twelve chances to clean up. Okay okay, fifteen! Fine! That's fair, and that's all you get. If you can't make it in fifteen tries, off you go . . . to Colorado! The perfect place for staying loaded.

Each week, all of the illegal drugs confiscated in the United States—at least those drugs the police and DEA don't keep for their own personal use—will be air-dropped into Colorado. That way, everyone can stay stoned, bombed, wasted, smashed, hammered, and fucked up around the clock on another new cable channel: Shitface Central. This is the real Rocky Mountain high.

Now, I've saved my favorite group for last. **The Maniacs and Crazy People.** The ones who live out where the buses don't run. And I always take care to distinguish between maniacs and crazy people. A maniac will beat nine people to death with a steel dildo. A crazy person will beat nine people to death with a steel dildo, but he'll be wearing a Bugs Bunny suit at the time.

So you can't put them all away. You have to keep some of them around just for the entertainment. Like the guy who tells you the King of Sweden is using his gallbladder as a radio transmitter to send anti-Semitic, lesbian meat loaf recipes to Marvin Hamlisch. A guy like that, you want to give him his own radio show.

No, the Maniac Farm will be used strictly for hopeless cases. Like a guy who gets a big tattoo on his chest of Madonna taking a shit. You know? Then he tells you that if he flexes certain muscles it looks like she's wipin' her ass. A guy like that, you wanna get him into custody as quickly as possible.

Now, for the Maniac Farm I think there's no question we have to go with Utah. Easy to fence, and right next to Wyoming and Colorado. And Colorado is right next to? Right, Kansas! And that means that *all four groups* of our most amusing citizens are now in one place. Except for the big electric fences. And, folks, I think I have another one of my really good ideas for cable TV. Gates! Small sliding gates in the fences.

Think what you have here. Four groups: degenerates, predators, crackheads, and fruitcakes. All separated by 900 miles of fence. And here's how you have some fun: every ten miles, you put a small, sliding gate in the fence. But—the gates are only ten inches wide, and they're only opened once a month. For seven seconds.

And you know something? Fuck cable, this stuff belongs on pay-per-view. Because if those gates are only open seven seconds a month, you are gonna have some mighty interesting people trying to be first on line. Deeply disturbed, armed, cranky lunatics on drugs! You know the ones: a lot of tattoos; a lot of teeth broken off at the gum line. The true face of America. And every time you open the gates a few of the more aggressive ones are gonna slip through. The crème de la crème. The alphas! They're gonna slip through, they're gonna find each other, and they're gonna cross-breed.

And pretty soon you'll have the American melting pot: child-killers, corpse-fuckers, drug zombies, and full-blown twelve-cylinder wackaloons. All wandering the landscape in search of truth. And fun. Just like now. Everyone will have guns, everyone will have drugs, and no one will be in charge. Just like now. But Social Security will be fully funded.

I'LL BE RIGHT BACK

I've never been impressed with people who tell me what they plan to do when they go to the bathroom. Doesn't that bother you? People who announce their intentions?

"I'll be right back, Trevor, I'm gonna take a shit."

"Never mind, Pietro! Do what you have to and leave me out of it. And please don't describe it when you get back."

[Time, among other things, passes.]

"Boy, you shoulda seen . . ."

"Never mind!"

"It set off the smoke alarm."

"Never mind!"

"The rest room attendant passed out."

I've never understood people who describe their bowel achievements. Nor have I much cared for it. Especially at a fine restaurant.

NOT EVERY EJACULATION DESERVES A NAME

Have you noticed that most people who are against abortion are people you wouldn't want to fuck in the first place? Conservatives are physically unattractive and morally inconsistent. They're obsessed with fetuses from conception to nine months, but after that they have no interest in you. None. No day care, no Head Start, no school lunch, no food stamps, no welfare, no nothin'. If you're preborn, you're fine; if you're preschool, you're fucked.

Once you leave the womb, conservatives don't care about you until you reach military age. Then you're just what they're looking for. Conservatives want live babies so they can raise them to be dead soldiers.

Pro-life. How can they be pro-life when they're killing doctors? What sort of moral philosophy is that? "We'll do anything to save a fetus, but we might have to kill it later on if it grows up to be a doctor"? They're not pro-life; they're antiwoman. Simple. They're afraid of women, and they don't like them. They believe a woman's primary role is to function as a brood mare for the State. If they think a fetus is more important than a woman, they should try getting a fetus to wash the shit stains out of their underwear. For no pay.

Pro-life. You don't see many white, antiabortion women volunteering to have black fetuses transplanted into their uteruses, do you? No. You don't see them adopting any crack babies, do you? No, that's something Jesus would do.

And you won't see many pro-lifers dousing themselves with kerosene and lighting themselves on fire. Remember the Buddhist monks in Vietnam? Morally committed religious people in Southeast Asia knew how to stage a protest: light yourself on fire! C'mon, you Christian crusaders, let's see a little smoke. Let's see if you can match that fire in your bellies.

Separate thought: Why is it when it's a human being it's called an abortion, and when it's a chicken it's called an omelet. Are we so much better than chickens? When did that happen? Name six ways we're better than chickens. See? No one can do it. You know why? Because chickens are decent people.

You don't see chickens hanging around in drug gangs, do you? No. You don't see chickens strappin' someone to a chair and hookin' up their nuts to a car battery. And when's the last time you heard about a chicken who came home from work and beat the shit out of his hen? Huh? It doesn't happen. You know why? Because chickens are decent people.

Back to abortion: The central question seems to be "Are fetuses human beings?" Well, if fetuses are human beings, why aren't they counted by the census? If fetuses are human beings, why is it there's no funeral following a miscarriage? If fetuses are human beings, why do people say, "We have two children and one on the way," instead of saying, "We have three children"?

Some people say life begins at conception; I say life began a billion years ago, and it's a continuous process. And actually, it goes back farther than that. What about the carbon atoms? Human life could not exist without carbon. So is it possible that maybe we shouldn't be burning all this coal? I don't mean to be picky, I'm just lookin' for a little consistency.

The hard-core pro-lifers tell us that life begins at fertilization, when the sperm fertilizes the egg. Which usually occurs a few minutes after the man says, "Sorry, honey, I was gonna pull out, but the phone startled me."

But even after fertilization it's still six or seven days before the egg reaches the uterus and pregnancy begins. And not every egg makes it. Eighty percent of a woman's fertilized eggs are rinsed out of her body once a month during those delightful few days she has. They end up on sanitary napkins, and yet they are fertilized eggs. So, what these antiabortion people are actually telling us is that any woman who's had more than one period is a serial killer. I don't mean to be picky, I'm just looking for a little consistency.

And speaking of consistency, Catholics—which I was until I reached the age of reason—Catholics and other Christians are against abortions, and they're against homosexuals. Well, who has less abortions than homosexuals? Here's an entire class of citizens guaranteed never to have an abortion, and the Catholics and Christians are just tossin' them aside. You'd think they'd be natural allies.

And regarding the Catholics, when I hear that the Pope and some of his "holy" friends have experienced their first pregnancies and labor pains, and raised a couple of children on minimum wage, I'll be glad to hear what they have to say about abortion. In the meantime, what they ought to do is tell these priests who took a vow of chastity to keep their hands off the altar boys. When Jesus said, "Suffer the little children come unto me," pedophilia is not what he was talking about. He had something else in mind.

I'VE GOT YOUR SANCTITY OF LIFE

One phrase that comes up quite a bit in abortion discussions is "sanctity of life." What about that? Do you think there's such a thing as sanctity of life? Personally, I think it's a bunch of shit. Who says life is sacred? God? Great, but if you read your history you know that God is one of the leading causes of death and has been for thousands of years. Hindus, Moslems, Christians, Jews, all taking turns killing one another, because God told them it was a good idea. The sword of God, the blood of the lamb, vengeance is mine. Millions of dead people. All because they gave the wrong answer to the God Question:

"Do you believe in God?"

"No."

BAM! Dead.

"How about you? Do you believe in God?"

"Yes."

"Do you believe in *my* God?"

"No."

BAM! Dead!

"My god has a bigger dick than your god."

For thousands of years all the bloodiest and most brutal wars have been based on religious hatred. Which, of course, is fine with me; any time "holy" people are killing one another, I'm a happy guy. But please, don't kill each other and then give me that shit about "sanctity of life." Even if there were such an absurd thing, I don't think you could blame it on God.

You know where the sanctity of life comes from? We made it up. You know why? Because we're alive. Self-interest! Living people have a strong incentive to promote the idea that somehow life is sacred. You don't see Bing Crosby runnin' around talking about this shit, do you? You don't hear much from Mussolini on the subject. And what's the latest from JFK? Not a goddamn thing! You know why? Because JFK, Mussolini, and Bing Crosby are all fuckin' dead. They're fuckin' dead, and dead people give less than a shit about the sanctity of life.

The only people who care about it are the living. So the whole thing grows out of a biased point of view. It's a self-serving, man-made bullshit story; one of those things we tell ourselves in order to feel noble. "Life is sacred." Makes us feel good. But let me ask you this: If everything that ever lived is dead, and everything alive is going to die, where does the sacred part come in? Can you help me on that?

Because even with all we preach about the sanctity of life, we don't practice it. Look at what we kill: Mosquitoes and flies, because they're pests. Lions and tigers, because it's fun. Chickens and pigs, because we're hungry. And people. We kill people. Because they're pests. And because it's fun!

And here's something else I noticed. Apparently, the sanctity of life doesn't apply to cancer cells, does it? You rarely see a bumper sticker that says Save the Tumors. Or I Brake for Advanced Melanoma. No. Viruses, molds, mildew, maggots, fungus, weeds, intestinal worms, *E. coli* bacteria, the crabs. Nothin' sacred about those things. Just us.

So, at best, the sanctity of life is a selective thing. We choose which forms of life we feel are sacred, and we get to kill the rest. Pretty neat deal. You know how we got it? We made the whole thing up! Same way we made up the death penalty. The sanctity of life, and the death penalty. We're such a versatile species.

READY OR NOT, HERE WE COME!

The latest disaster for the solar system is that the United States has decided go to Mars. And, of course, later we intend to colonize deep space with our Salad Shooters and Snot Candy and microwave hot dogs. But let me ask you this: What are we going to tell the Intergalactic Council the first time one of our young women throws her newborn baby out of a seventh-story window? And how do we explain to the Near-Stellar Trade Confederation that our representative was late for the meeting because his breakfast was cold, and he had to spend thirty minutes beating the shit out of his wife?

Do you think the elders of the Universal Board of Wisdom will understand that it's simply because of quaint local customs that over 80 million of our women have had their clitorises and labia cut off and their vulvas sewn shut in order to make them more marriageable and unable to derive pleasure from sex and thus never be a threat to stray from their husbands' beds?

Can't you just sense how eager the rest of the universe is for us to show up?

NEVER HEARD OF HIM!

You ever notice that suddenly overnight someone you never heard of becomes a big celebrity; and you never heard their name before? Ever? And you think, Who the fuck is this? How can this happen without me noticing? Usually it's because the person is in some line of work you're not interested in, like popular music or network television. They're on some TV show you wouldn't watch unless you were strapped in bed in a nuthouse, but suddenly there are big magazine articles about them, and they're on Leno and Letterman. Don't you feel really good two years later when they've completely disappeared; gone back to the supermarket? It's very satisfying.

SHORT TAKES

Have you ever been on trial for murder? It's weird. You don't know what to do with yourself. Singing is out. Mostly I stare at the judge.

Is a vegetarian permitted to eat animal crackers?

I've figured out how to commit the perfect double murder. You pick one person up by the ankles and beat the other person to death with him. They both die, and there's no murder weapon.

Peg Leg Bates's wife is one person who never had to wait for the other shoe to drop.

Have you ever had a hatchet go right through your face? Not a glancing blow, but a full-on shot, deep into your forehead? Deep enough so you can shake your head and the hatchet doesn't fall out? It's the strangest feeling. Because just after the hatchet goes in, and before there's any pain, you can feel a gentle puff of cool air on your brain. It feels good. But since it's the only way to get that feeling, I try not to get too hung up on it.

Wouldn't it be great if just one of these times at Daytona or Indianapolis, because of accidents and various mechanical failures, there were simply no cars at all left to finish the race? What color flag would they wave then?

Suggested bumper sticker We Are the Proud Parents of a Child Whose Self-Esteem Is Sufficient that He Doesn't Need Us Advertising His Minor Scholastic Achievements on the Bumper of Our Car.

When did they pass a law that says the people who make my sandwich have to be wearing gloves? I'm not comfortable with this; I don't want glove residue all over my food. It's not sanitary. Who knows where these gloves have been? Let's get back to human hands making sandwiches for human beings.

As you swim the river of life, do the breast stroke. It helps to clear the turds from your path.

YOU PICK IT, I'LL LICK IT.

Have you ever tried to throw away an old wastebasket? You can't do it. People keep bringing it back: "Here, Howie, I found your wastebasket in the garbage." Apparently, you have to completely destroy a wastebasket in order to convince people you really don't want it anymore.

In Los Angeles, there's a hotline for people in denial. So far no one has called.

Just once I'd like to see a high-speed funeral procession. A hearse, some flower cars, and a bunch of limousines tearin' ass through town at 70 miles an hour, on their way to the cemetery. Maybe someday a race-car driver will put that in his will.

You know a business that doesn't lend itself too easily to the Internet? Pay toilets.

Here's something I consider a crime against society: women with hyphenated names. Hey, lady, pick a fuckin' name, will you?

"Hi. I'm Emily Jarrikov-Fortescu."

"Hi. I'm George Jerkmeoff-Fuckyoutoo!"

Attention women: You don't attain self-esteem or personal dignity by adding a name to your name. Modern feminists apparently think hyphenation is a radical act. It's not. Castrating a man in a parking lot with a Coke bottle is a radical act. Hyphenating your name is pretentious, middle-class bullshit.

No one ever knows what's next, but they always do it.

You know what they don't have? A really good French football player. You never hear about some guy named Pierre La Doux smashing through the line of scrimmage and picking up a first down. Why is that?

The only hip thing left to do in America is to blow up a building. Believe me.

Fun Stuff: Walk into a gun store, buy three guns and a bunch of ammunition. Then ask them if they have any ski masks.

I have a very inexpensive security system. If someone breaks into my house, I run next door and throw a brick through my neighbor's window. That sets off his alarm and when the police arrive I direct them to my house.

As Asian immigrants become more completely assimilated into American society over the next few generations, their standards of hard work and academic excellence will drop, and they will feel more at home here.

Some teenage girls delay getting abortions because they're afraid to comply with the parental notification laws. Especially if one of the parents also happens to be the father of the child.

Here's a plastic surgery option: have one nostril sewn shut. I feel like I might be ready for that.

Regarding the Pledge of Allegiance and other patriotic nonsense: what does placing your hand over your heart have to do with anything? Or removing your hat when the flag is passing by? Am I missing something?

True Stuff: There is actually a Tow-Truck Hall of Fame.

I just realized I haven't been scared in a really long time.

Didn't the first guy who wore a sombrero realize it was completely impractical when eating pussy?

I don't understand motivation books. What happened here? Suddenly everybody needs to be motivated? It's a fairly simple thing: either you want to do something or you don't; there's no mystery. Besides, if you're motivated enough to go to the store to buy a motivation book, aren't you motivated enough to do that? So, you don't need the book. Put it back. Tell the clerk, "Fuck you, I'm goin' home. I'm already motivated."

Safety Tip: Always wear a leather glove when giving a porcupine a hand job.

You know a word you don't hear enough anymore? Hosiery.

SPORTS SHOULD BE FIXED: SECOND HALF

Basketball: No Harm, No Fun

Continuing my attempt to improve professional sports with basketball, once again I propose to make the game more exciting by changing the rules. But in this case I concentrate less on violence and injuries and a bit more on spicing up the game.

To begin with, basketball would be faster and a whole lot more exciting if they had a three-second shot clock. Never mind that passing shit; as soon as the ball is in play, get that son of a bitch up in the air. I didn't pay to watch a game of catch, I'm lookin' for a 700-point ball game.

Here's another good suggestion: all free throws should be taken as jump shots. Players should have to drive from half-court, pull up at the foul line, and shoot the jumper. Much more exciting. And speaking of foul shots, I would retain the six-foul limit, but I would increase it to six fouls per quarter per man. This way you avoid that stupid foul-trouble shit and keep the stars on the court.

Next, I think before anyone touches a rebound, it should be allowed to bounce one time and then let the players fight over it. And if a rebound goes into the stands, the spectator who catches the ball should be allowed to shoot two free throws for his team. Get the fans involved.

And here's something interesting no one else has thought of: when one of those hyperactive players dives into the crowd trying to keep a ball from going out-of-bounds, he should have to stay and sit in the stands for three minutes. Like the penalty box in hockey. And by the way, when is one of those diving, Charlie Hustle guys gonna break his fuckin' neck on a chair? You just don't see enough of that sort of thing.

Here's another good idea: fifty points for any shot made from beyond the half-court line. It would be great for those lopsided games in the fourth quarter. And I'll guarantee you some guys would practice that shot and get good at it. Then they could just hang around half-court the whole game, and when the teams switch baskets at halftime, all they'd have to do is turn around and face the other way.

Something else I'll bet has never come up at a meeting of the rules committee: bonus points for any shot that goes in the basket after bouncing off another guy's head. Fifty points if it's a teammate, 100 if it's an opponent. Believe me, you'd see a lot of good fights. And, actually, the brain injuries alone would make this one well worth trying.

Two more suggestions. If a team falls behind by more than 15 points, they have to let their girlfriends come in and help them on defense. It's just the kind of motivation these macho duds need to keep the games close.

And last—and, honestly, I do not think this is excessive—during overtime periods I would allow the players to use small personal weapons, excluding firearms. I think knives and blackjacks, employed sparingly, would contribute to some rousing finishes in these evenly matched games.

DON'T BLAME THE LEADERS

You, the People

In the midst of all my bitching, you might've noticed that I never complain about politicians. I leave that to others. And there's no shortage of volunteers; everyone complains about politicians. Everyone says they suck.

But where do people think these politicians come from? They don't fall out of the sky; they don't pass through a membrane from a separate reality. They come from American homes, American families, American schools, American churches, and American businesses. And they're elected by American voters. This is what our system produces, folks. This is the best we can do. Let's face it, we have very little to work with. Garbage in, garbage out.

Ignorant citizens elect ignorant leaders, it's as simple as that. And term limits don't help. All you do is get a brand new bunch of ignorant leaders.

So maybe it's not the politicians who suck; maybe it's something else. Like the public. That would be a nice realistic campaign slogan for somebody: "The public sucks. Elect me." Put the blame where it belongs: on the people.

Because if everything is really the fault of politicians, where are all the bright, honest, intelligent Americans who are ready to step in and replace them? Where are these people hiding? The truth is, we don't have people like that. Everyone's at the mall, scratching his balls and buying sneakers with lights in them. And complaining about the politicians.

Vote? No!

For myself, I have solved this political dilemma in a very direct way. On Election Day, I stay home. Two reasons: first of all, voting is meaningless; this country was bought and paid for a long time ago. That empty shit they shuffle around and repackage every four years doesn't mean a thing.

Second, I don't vote, because I firmly believe that if you vote, you have no right to complain. I know some people like to twist that around and say, "If you *don't* vote, you have no right to complain."

But where's the logic in that? Think it through: if you vote, and you elect dishonest, incompetent politicians, and they screw things up, then you're responsible for what they've done. You voted them in. You caused the problem. You have no right to complain.

I, on the other hand, who did not vote—who, in fact, did not even leave the house on Election Day—am in no way responsible for what these politicians have done and have every right to complain about the mess you created. Which I had nothing to do with. Why can't people see that?

Now, I realize last year you folks had another one of those really swell presidential elections you treasure so much. That was nice. I'm sure you had a good time, and I'm sure that everyone's life has now improved. But I'm happy to tell you that on Election Day I stayed home. And I did essentially what you did. The only difference is when I got finished masturbating I had something to show for it.

The 20th Century World-Hostility Scoreboard

The following is a list of hostilities that took place in the 20th Century among the civilized peoples of the world. The uncivilized were unable to provide reliable statistics.

2	world wars		691	wars of honor
250	civil wars		296	declared wars
311	holy wars		856	undeclared wars
1	cold war		4	brushfire wars
516	wars of liberation		2	vest-pocket wars
331	wars of containment		413	limited wars

1,987	acts of war	946	carpet bombings
7,756	warlike acts	4,288	threats to security
88	police actions	286	popular uprisings
2	nuclear attacks	1,877	areas of unrest
6,578	government massacres	622	strife-torn regions
4	holocausts	165	internal upheavals
943	jihads	745	political repressions
693	pogroms	12,194	acts of sabotage
614	longterm persecutions	1,633	swift reprisals
12,111	acts of treachery	818	armed resistances
575	betrayals of the masses	639	repressive measures
958	grabs for power	1,126	violent outbursts
400	putsches	9,876	mass detentions
50	total enslavements	11,904	guerilla operations
837	partial enslavements	3,466	suicide missions
4	total genocides	823	slaughters
461	partial genocides	1,200	bloodbaths
13,658	cease-fire violations	43,096	atrocities
3,115	boundary disputes	161	reigns of terror
1,432	border clashes	715	rebellions
3,047	social conflicts	28	revolutions
798	sectarian rivalries	21	counterrevolutions
13,678	civil disturbances	746	coups

745	countercoups	515	regional tinderboxes
457	insurgencies	818	military flashpoints
458	counterinsurgencies	2,415	heated exchanges
4,622	covert operations	911	shows of force
3,422	direct interventions	668	heightenings of tension
617	enemy incursions	735	deliberate provocations
13	measured responses	921	military confrontations
295	commando strikes	639	dangerous escalations
694	retaliatory raids	3,721	terrorist bombings
844	surprise attacks	438	preemptive strikes
236	protective reactions	630	outside aggressions
2,155	frontal assaults	8,571	violent disturbances
213	responses in kind	646	surgical strikes
17,867	hostile incidents	4,392	diplomatic deadlocks
4,756	belligerent moves	82,879	ultimatums
938	naked aggressions	788,969,747	heated arguments
849	foreign adventures	823,285,571	shoving matches
601	overseas entanglements	917,704,296	fistfights
307	arms races	942,759,050	snotty phone calls
98	international powder kegs		

That's how we did, folks. Not a bad record, although we could have done better, considering the number of fools in our ranks.

ROCKETS AND PENISES IN THE PERSIAN GULF

History Lesson

I'd like to talk a little about that "war" we had in the Persian Gulf. Remember that? The big war in the Persian Gulf? Lemme tell you what was goin' on.

Naturally, you can forget all that entertaining fiction about having to defend the model democracy those lucky Kuwaitis get to live under. And for the moment you can also put aside the very real, periodic need Americans have for testing their new weapons on human flesh. And also, just for the fun of it, let's ignore George Bush's obligation to protect the oil interests of his family and friends. There was another, much more important, consideration at work. Here's what really happened.

Dropping a Load for Uncle Sam

The simple fact is that America was long overdue to drop high explosives on helpless civilians; people who have no argument with us whatsoever. After all, it had been awhile, and the hunger gnaws. Remember that's our specialty: picking on countries that have marginally effective air forces. Yugoslavia is another, more recent, example.

Surfing Unnecessary

But all that aside, let me tell you what I liked about that Gulf War: it was the first war that appeared on every television channel, including cable. And even though the TV show consisted largely of

Pentagon war criminals displaying maps and charts, it got very good ratings. And that makes sense, because we like war. We're a warlike people. We can't stand not to be fucking with someone. We couldn't wait for the Cold War to end so we could climb into the big Arab sandbox and play with our nice new toys. We enjoy war.

And one reason we enjoy it is that we're good at it. You know why we're good at it? Because we get a lot of practice. This country is only 200 years old, and already we've had ten major wars. We average a major war every twenty years. So we're good at it!

And it's just as well we are, because we're not very good at anything else. Can't build a decent car anymore. Can't make a TV set, a cell phone, or a VCR. Got no steel industry left. No textiles. Can't educate our young people. Can't get health care to our old people. But we can bomb the shit outta your country, all right. We can bomb the shit outta your country!

If You're Brown, You're Goin' Down

Especially if your country is full of brown people. Oh, we like that, don't we? That's our hobby now. But it's also our new job in the world: bombing brown people. Iraq, Panama, Grenada, Libya. You got some brown people in your country? Tell 'em to watch the fuck out, or we'll goddamn bomb them!

Well, who were the last white people you can remember that we bombed? In fact, can you remember *any* white people we ever bombed? The Germans! That's it! Those are the only ones. And that was only because they were tryin' to cut in on our action. They wanted to dominate the world. Bullshit! That's our job. That's our fuckin' job.

But the Germans are ancient history. These days, we only bomb brown people. And not because they're cutting in on our action; we do it because they're brown. Even those Serbs we bombed in Yugoslavia aren't *really* white, are they? Naaah! They're sort of down near the swarthy end of the white spectrum. Just brown enough to bomb. I'm still waiting for the day we bomb the English. People who really deserve it.

A Disobedient American

Now, you folks might've noticed, I don't feel about that Gulf War the way we were instructed to feel about it by the United States government. My mind doesn't work that way. You see, I've got this real moron thing I do, it's called "thinking." And I guess I'm not a very good American, because I like to form my own opinions; I don't just roll over when I'm told. Most Americans roll over on command. Not me. There are certain rules I observe.

Believe You Me

My first rule: Never believe anything anyone in authority says. None of them. Government, police, clergy, the corporate criminals. None of them. And neither do I believe anything I'm told by the media, who, in the case of the Gulf War, functioned as little more than unpaid employees of the Defense Department, and who, most of the time, operate as an unofficial public relations agency for government and industry.

I don't believe in any of them. And I have to tell you, folks, I don't really believe very much in my country either. I don't get all choked up about yellow ribbons and American flags. I see them as symbols, and I leave them to the symbol-minded.

Show Us Your Dick

I also look at war itself a little differently from most. I see it largely as an exercise in dick-waving. That's really all it is: a lot of men standing around in a field waving their dicks at one another. Men, insecure about the size of their penises, choose to kill one another.

That's also what all that moron athlete bullshit is about, and what that macho, male posturing and strutting around in bars and locker rooms represents. It's called "dick fear." Men are terrified that their dicks are inadequate, and so they have to "compete" in order to feel better about themselves. And since war is the ultimate competition, essentially men are killing one another in order to improve their genital self-esteem.

You needn't be a historian or a political scientist to see the Bigger Dick Foreign Policy Theory at work. It goes like this: "What? They have bigger dicks? Bomb them!" And of course, the bombs, the rockets, and the bullets are all shaped like penises. Phallic weapons. There's an unconscious need to project the national penis into the affairs of others. It's called "fucking with people."

Show Us Your Bush

So, as far as I'm concerned, that whole thing in the Persian Gulf was nothing more than one big dick-waving cockfight. In this particular case, Saddam Hussein questioned the size of George Bush's dick. And George Bush had been called a wimp for so long, he apparently felt the need to act out his manhood fantasies by sending America's white children to kill other people's brown children. Clearly the worst *kind* of wimp.

Even his name, "Bush," as slang, is *related* to the genitals without actually being the genitals. A bush is sort of a passive, secondary sex characteristic. It's even used as a slang term for women: "Hey, pal, how's the bush in this area?" I can't help thinking, if this president's name had been George Boner . . . well, he might have felt a little better about himself, and he wouldn't have had to kill all those children. Too bad he couldn't locate his manhood.

Premature Extraction

Actually, when you think about it, this country has had a manhood problem for some time. You can tell by the language we use; language always gives us away. What did we do wrong in Vietnam? We "pulled out"! Not a very manly thing to do. No. When you're fucking people, you're supposed to stay with it and fuck them good; fuck them to death; hang in there and keep fucking them until they're all fucking dead.

But in Vietnam what happened was by accident we left a few women and children alive, and we haven't felt good about ourselves since. That's why in the Persian Gulf, George Bush had to say, "This will not be another Vietnam." He actually said, "this time we're *going all the way*." Imagine. An American president using the sexual slang of a thirteen-year-old to describe his foreign policy.

And, of course, when it got right down to it, he *didn't* "go all the way." Faced with going into Baghdad he punked out. No balls. Just Bush. Instead, he applied sanctions, so he'd be sure that an extra half a million brown children would die. And so his oil buddies could continue to fill their pockets.

If you want to know what happened in the Persian Gulf, just remember the first names of the two men who ran that war: Dick Cheney and Colin Powell. Dick and colon. Someone got fucked in the ass. And those brown people better make sure they keep their pants on, because Dick and Colin have come back for an encore.

OLD AND STINGY

Here's something that pisses me off: retired people who don't want to pay local property taxes, because they say it's not their grandchildren who go to the schools. Mean-spirited retirees usually from out of state. Cheap, selfish, old Bush voters. The ones I read about were in Arizona. AARP members. They take a shit the size of a peanut and think it's an accomplishment.

And it's not like these retirement people can't afford the tax money. Not all old people are as dependent on Social Security checks as they'd like you to think. Some of them get all kinds of checks: Social Security, the VA, private pensions, government pensions. They also have stock dividends, bank interest, and whatever else they've managed to squeeze out of the system.

And still they begrudge their local property taxes simply because their own fucked-up, cross-eyed grandchildren aren't gonna use the schools. Fuck 'em! I say pay your taxes and die like everybody else. I hope they choke on an early-bird dinner.

SHORT TAKES

What exactly is wrong with inmates running the asylum? It seems to me they're in an ideal position to know just what's needed.

HOORAY FOR MOST THINGS!

When it comes to my organs, I've decided to donate only my prostate and testicles, with the stipulation that they go to one of those lovely feminists.

Here's something no one ever wrote before: "Big bats down to one five, five over cross, up the thingo. Nose, baseball, hieroglyphics, hopscotch, pouch. Inevitably, two four eight, four eight, four eight, four eighth. I. I with a two, two, two. Three. Four. Five. Down here, Mother, we're all home now. So long, Jill. Beep beep. Hungry, hungry. Are you? I couldn't stand it. Not in my house. Up yours, too, Don. He's packin' them in! We'll all try it. Fifty-fifty? Okay, but not me." No one ever wrote that before. Not even Shakespeare. I'm proud of that.

Civilization began its downhill path the day some guy first uttered the words, "A man's gotta do what a man's gotta do."

Have you ever been in the middle of a nice, pleasant dream, when you suddenly wake up and realize someone is trying to kill you? You know what I do? I go back to sleep.

They say if you live to be 100 your lucky number goes up by one.

Near as I can tell, "jack shit" and "diddly-squat" are roughly the same amount.

What do you think about some guy who hears a voice in his head that tells him to kill his entire family, and he does it? Is that the only thing these voices ever tell paranoid guys to do? Kill people? Doesn't a voice ever say, "Go take a shit on the salad bar at Wendy's!" Doesn't a voice tell a guy to take out his dick on the merry-go-round? Actually, some guys do take out their dicks on the merry-go-round. But usually it's their own idea.

In the old days white people used to put black greasepaint on their faces and perform menstrual shows. That must have been really interesting.

When I first heard the song "Don't Worry, Be Happy," I realized it was exactly the kind of mindless philosophy that Americans would respond to. It would make a great national motto. Right along with Me First.

Little-Known Fact: When the stock exchange closes, the guy who comes out on the balcony with that big hammer slams it on the head of the person who lost the most money that day.

America has too many fake Irish pubs. Giving your bar an Irish name doesn't make it a pub. The word pub is earned the hard way: tons and tons of puke and thousands of shattered cheekbones.

McDonald's breakfast for under a dollar is actually more expensive than that. You have to factor in the cost of bypass surgery.

May I make it clear that I don't care what country the pope is in? I'm really not interested. All the pope ever does is go around to places where people make six dollars a year and tell them to have more children. Isn't that bright? And responsible! And compassionate. Such a bright, responsible, compassionate man. If the pope wants to travel around, flaunting his wealth and encouraging poor people to have children, let him do it privately. And for God's sake, keep it off television. The pope is not news.

No one who has ever had "Taps" played for them has been able to hear it.

Although it's true blondes have more fun, it's important to remember that they also have more venereal disease.

If you watch a sitcom carefully, you can see that it's really nothing more than a series of doors opening and closing with a series of jackoffs entering and exiting.

Here's a great idea: A roach spray that doesn't kill the roach, but, instead, fills him with self-doubt as to whether or not he's in the right house.

I'm sure looters don't call it looting. They probably think of it as extreme shopping.

FUCK THE POLITICAL CENTER

America got what it deserved in Elvis Presley: a big fat, drug-addict squealer. And don't get me wrong, there's nothing wrong with being a drug addict. But he wasn't even addicted to a cool drug like heroin. It was medicine. Fuckin' doctor drugs.

One good reason for maintaining only a small circle of friends is that three out of four murders are committed by people who know the victim.

If you live on the wrong side of the tracks but get up on the right side of the bed, do those things cancel each other out? Probably not.

Professional soldiers are people who die for a living.

Here's Some Fun: Go into a photography shop and ask the man if you can buy the pictures of the other people in the window. Say, "How much for that heavy-set couple?" I guarantee they'll stare at you a long time. In fact, they might even back up several feet.

Whenever they say someone got hit by a "stray bullet" I wonder about the choice of words. It seems to me the bullet isn't stray at all. It's doing exactly what physics predicts: travelling in a straight line. What's so stray about that?

AT LEAST EAT A FUCKIN' LIMA BEAN, WILL YA?

Beverly Hills has a new restaurant for bulimia victims. It's called The Scarf and Barf. Originally, they were gonna call it The Fork and Bucket. Thank God, once again good taste prevailed in Beverly Hills.

They're also planning a restaurant for anorexics, but again, having trouble with the name. It's a toss-up between The Empty Plate and Lonesome Chef. I suggested Start Without Me, Guys.

Tell you the truth, I don't feel sorry for an anorexic. Do you? Some rich cunt doesn't wanna eat? Fuck her! Don't eat. I give a shit. Like I'm supposed to be concerned.

"I don't wanna eat!"

"Go fuck yourself! Why don't you lie down in front of a railroad train after you don't eat?"

What kind of a goddamn disease is anorexia, anyway? "I don't wanna eat!" How do we come up with this shit? Where do we get our values?

Bulimia. There's another all-American disease. This has gotta be the only country in the world where some people are digging in the dumpster for a peach pit while other people eat a nice meal and puke it up intentionally. Where do we get our values?

FACE-TO-FACE WITH THE CLOCK

I remember when they tried to teach me to tell time as a little boy. What they didn't know, of course, was that you don't tell time; time tells you. Still they tried.

"Now, George, the big hand is on . . ."

"I don't have a big hand. Both my hands are little."

"Never mind. Just look at the clock."

And I did. It was wonderful. I love the face of a clock. To me, there is great emotion attached to the face of a clock. A conventional analog clock.

Digital clocks are all right in their place, I suppose, but they lack the friendly spatial relationships that exist between the hands and the numerals on an analog clock.

There's a psychological component: to me, the first half of any hour, as the minute hand falls from 12 to 6, passes a lot more quickly than the second half, when it has to struggle upward, fighting gravity all the way.

I'll say this much: If I had only half an hour to live, I'd want it to be the second half. I just know it would last a little longer.

GOD HAS GOTTA GO

I make fun of people who are religious, because I think they're fundamentally weak. But I want you to know that on a personal level, when it comes to believing in God, I tried. I really, really tried. I tried to believe there is a God, who created us in his own image, loves us very much, and keeps a close eye on things.

I tried to believe it. But I have to tell you, the longer you live, the more you look around, the more you realize . . . something is fucked. Something is wrong. War, disease, death, destruction, hunger, filth, poverty, torture, crime, corruption, and the Ice Capades. Something is definitely wrong.

If this is the best God can do, I'm not impressed. Results like these do not belong on the résumé of a supreme being. This is the kind of stuff you'd expect from an office temp with a bad attitude. In any well-managed universe, this guy would've been out on his all-powerful ass a long time ago.

So, if there is a God—if there is—I think reasonable people might agree he's at least incompetent and maybe, just maybe, he doesn't give a shit. Which I admire in a person, and which would explain a lot of his results.

I Got the Sun in the Mornin'

So, rather than becoming just another mindless, religious robot, blindly believing that everything is in the hands of some spooky, in-competent father figure who doesn't give a shit, I decided to look around for something else to worship. Something I could really count on. And immediately, I thought of the sun. It happened in an instant. Overnight, I became a sun worshipper.

Well, not overnight; you can't see the sun in the dark. But first thing the next morning, I became a sun worshipper. For several reasons: First of all, I can see the sun. Unlike some other gods I could mention, I can actually see the sun. I'm big on that. If I can see something, it kind of helps the credibility.

Every day I can see the sun as it gives me everything I need: heat, light, food, flowers in the park, reflections on the lake. An occasional skin cancer, but, hey! At least there are no crucifixions. And we sun worshippers don't go around killing other people simply because they don't agree with us.

Sun worship is fairly simple. There's no mystery, no miracles, no pageantry, no one asks for money, there are no songs to learn, and we don't have a special building where we all gather once a week to compare clothing. And the best thing about the sun . . . it never tells me I'm unworthy. It doesn't tell me I'm a bad person who needs to be saved. Hasn't said an unkind word. Treats me fine.

Praying on My Mind

So I worship the sun. But I don't pray to the sun. You know why? Because I wouldn't presume on our friendship. It's not polite. I've often thought people treat God rather rudely. Trillions and trillions of prayers every day, asking and pleading and begging for favors. "Do this; give me that; I need this; I want that." And most of this praying takes place on Sunday, his day off! It's not nice, and it's no way to treat a friend.

But still people do pray and they pray for many different things. And that's all right with me. I say, pray for anything you want. Pray for anything. But . . . what about the Divine Plan? Remember that? The Divine Plan? A long time ago, God came up with a Divine Plan. He gave it a lot of thought, he decided it was a good plan, and he put it into practice. And for billions and billions of years the Divine Plan has been doing just fine.

But now you come along and pray for something. Well, suppose the thing you're praying for isn't in God's Divine Plan? What do you want him to do? Change his plan? Just for you? Isn't that sort of arrogant? It's a Divine Plan! What good is being God if every rundown schmuck with a two-dollar prayer book can come along and fuck with your plan?

And here's another problem you might encounter. Suppose your prayers aren't answered? What do you do then? What do you say? "Well, it's God's will. Thy will be done"? Fine. But if it's God's will, and he's going to do what he wants anyway, why bother praying in the first place? Doesn't it seem like a big waste of time? Couldn't you just skip the praying part and go straight to "his will"? It's all very confusing to me.

To Each His Own

So, to get around all this, I decided to worship the sun. But as I said, I don't pray to the sun. You know who I pray to? Joe Pesci. Two reasons. First of all, I think he's a pretty good actor. To me, that counts. Second, he looks like a guy who can get things done. Joe doesn't fuck around. In fact, he came through on a couple of things that God was having trouble with. For years I asked God to do something about my noisy neighbor's barking dog. Nothing happened. But Joe Pesci? He straightened that shit out with one visit. It's amazing what you can accomplish with a simple piece of athletic equipment.

So, I've been praying to Joe for a couple of years now, and I've noticed something. I've noticed that all the prayers I used to offer to God and all the prayers I now offer to Joe Pesci are being answered at about the same 50 percent rate. Half the time I get what I want, half the time I don't. Same as God. Fifty-fifty. Same as the four-leaf clover, the horseshoe, the wishing well, and the rabbit's foot. Same as the mojo man, or the voodoo lady who tells you your fortune by squeezing a goat's testicles. It's all the same, fifty-fifty. So just pick a superstition you like, sit back, make a wish, and enjoy yourself.

Tell Me a Story, Daddy

And for those of you who look to the Bible for its moral lessons and literary qualities, I have a couple of other stories I'd like to recommend. You might want to try "The Three Little Pigs." That's a good one, it has a nice happy ending. Then there's "Little Red Riding Hood," although it does have that one X-rated part where the Big Bad Wolf actually eats the grandmother. Which I didn't care for.

And finally, I've always drawn a great deal of moral comfort from

Humpty Dumpty. The part I like best: "All the king's horses and all the king's men couldn't put Humpty Dumpty back together again." That's because there is no Humpty Dumpty. And there is no God. None, not one, never was. No God. Sorry.

BULLETS FOR BELIEVERS

I don't worry about guns in school. You know what I'm happy about? Guns in church! This is a terrific development, isn't it? And finally it's here! I'm so happy. I prayed for this. Oddly enough, I actually prayed for this. And I predicted it, too.

A couple of years ago I said that pretty soon there'd be some fuckin' yo-yo Christian with a Bible and a rifle who'd go apeshit in a church and kill six people. And the media would refer to him as a "disgruntled worshiper." I had no idea it would be a non-Christian. That's a really nice touch.

And my hat is off to the people of Texas for once again leading the way when it comes to the taking of human life. Texans are always in the vanguard of this important activity, and here they are again, setting a good example, showing the way. And finally they're going after the right people: the churchgoers. Let's face it, folks. They're askin' for it. They just want to be with Jesus. Give them a helping hand.

"Wanna see the Lord?" BANG! "Off you go!" BANG! "Are you a Christian?" BANG! "Say hello to Jesus!"

Give 'em a Christian helping hand. Don't think they wouldn't do the same for you. They don't call themselves "Christian soldiers" for nothing.

THE LATE-NIGHT NEWS

✱ The Supreme Court has reversed a lower court ruling which had let stand a Circuit Court decision allowing an injunction that restrained a defendant from contesting a court order forcing him to show cause why he should not be enjoined from suing his lawyer.

✱ A government witness who has been demanding twenty-four-hour protection today was given a roll-on deodorant.

✱ A woman who left her two-year-old son at a day care center yesterday morning says that when she returned to pick him up in the afternoon he was completely grown. Day care officials are crediting the hot-lunch program.

✱ Here are the results of the Blind Person's Golf Tournament. The winner was Johnny Dowling, with 2,829 strokes, just enough to beat Larry Powell, who lost any chance he may have had when he took a 612 on the final hole, including 115 separate putts.

✱ A priest who has performed over 300 exorcisms was eaten today by a green boogeyman.

✱ Twenty-one patrons of a Miami bar suffered numerous gunshot wounds to their feet and ankles as two armed dwarfs ran amok in a downtown tavern. Police say the two tiny men entered the bar riding horsey-back, and things got out of hand when the one on the bottom began to get drunk. In addition to the many foot wounds, extensive damage to the baseboards and electrical outlets was also reported.

✳ Mary Pierce, a woman who claimed she was filled with great love for everyone in the world, was killed today by a man who says he didn't know that.

✳ An unregistered nurse in Phoenix has been arrested for sending obscene get-well cards.

✳ In a bizarre accident, a man who looks like Dean Martin ran over and killed a man who resembles Jerry Lewis. Police spokesman Dave Brewster, who looks like Sammy Davis Jr., said they can find no significance.

✳ The international sword-swallowing championships were held in Sweden yesterday. The judges say the level of competition was especially fierce this year, and they will announce the winners as soon as they are able to remove them from the platform.

✳ Hollywood film star Vicki Lick, and her husband, Mark Stain, have called it quits after a seventeen-minute honeymoon in a pew in the back of the church.

✳ And finally, on the lighter side: *The Guinness Book of World Records* announced today that Harold Twirlfine of Boston has amassed the world's largest collection of chocolate pudding. Twirlfine, a carnival organist, has over 6,000 separate servings on display in his living room. He says that on many of the older servings an almost impenetrable skin has now formed, and in some cases the pudding has pulled completely away from the side of the dish. This has caused the formation of huge crevices where Twirlfine now stores part of his award-winning collection of Raisinets.

But Twirlfine's feat is nothing compared to the largest single mass of Jell-O in the world. That title belongs to the good citizens of Lemon Lime, Minnesota, who last year poured 200,000 boxes of Jell-O powder into the lake. Most of the locals are happy with the results; however, some people diving at the lake's shallow end have injured their heads on large pieces of fruit cocktail.

I NEVER FUCKED A 10

I never fucked a "10," but one night I fucked five 2s. And I think that ought to count. It ought to go down in my record as a positive achievement. But here's something I'm *really* proud of: I never fucked a 1. Well, I never got drunk enough. You have to swallow a lot of chemicals to even *talk* to a 1, much less actually fuck one.

Of course, some guys will fuck anybody. We know that. There's always one guy in every crowd who'll go,

"Hey, guys! Look! Let's fuck her!"

"That's a coat rack, Bob."

"So?"

Some guys will fuck anybody. Not me. Not anymore. Not since herpes and AIDS have been floating around. I'm playin' it safe these days. In fact, I'm being so careful I've stopped jerking off. You never know where your hand has been.

But if you're one of these guys who's still happily bashing the candle, I strongly suggest that you practice safe-sex masturbation. Don't take chances. If you're going to lie in bed and pretend you're fucking some unsuspecting female, for God's sake use a condom. It doesn't take much time out of your fantasy to get up and go over to the dresser and get a condom. She's not goin' anywhere, that's for sure! In fact, if you handle your fantasy correctly, you can probably talk her into goin' over and gettin' the condom for you.

SHORT TAKES

To spice up the Miss America contest, I think they ought to make the losers keep coming back until they win. Wouldn't that get spooky-looking after about thirty years? How would you like to see some seventy-year-old woman in a bathing suit?
   "I'd like everyone in the world to live in peace and harmony."
   "Fine. Sit down before you fall down. And pick up all those fuckin' batons!"

The Muslims observe their sabbath on Friday, the Jews observe on Saturday, and the Christians on Sunday. By the time Monday rolls around God is completely fuckin' worn out.

A lot of times when a package says Open Other End, I purposely open the end where it says that.

Looking back, I realize that my life has been a series of incidents where one person has said to another, "Get this asshole outta here!"

In the doggie dictionary, under "bow wow" it says, "See 'arf arf.'"

You know what you never see? A black guy with buckteeth.

When you look at the average American you realize there's nothing nature enjoys more than a good joke.

The future will soon be a thing of the past.

Can't we silence these Christian athletes who thank Jesus whenever they win and never mention his name when they lose? You never hear them say, "Jesus made me drop the ball," or, "The good Lord tripped me up behind the line of scrimmage." According to Christian athletes, Jesus is undefeated. Meanwhile, a lot of these Holy assholes are in sixth place. Maybe it's one of those miracles we hear so much about.

How come the Midwest is in the United States, and the Mideast is way the fuck overseas somewhere?

On Thanksgiving, most people give thanks for the things they have. Not me, I use Thanksgiving to ask for more things.

I think if a person doesn't immediately answer a public page in an airport, the paging should get increasingly hostile each time it is repeated. Until finally they're saying, "Goddammit, would the miserable jackoff calling himself David Klosterman please pick up the fuckin' white courtesy phone?"

Regarding these famous boxers who make comebacks when they're in their forties, don't you wish one of them would get killed in the ring? Just for a goof?

Here's a good example of practical humor, but you have to be in the right place. When a local television reporter is doing one of those on-the-street reports at the scene of a news story, usually you'll see some onlookers in the background of the shot, waving and trying to be seen on television. Go over and stand with them but don't wave. Just stand perfectly still and, without attracting attention, move your lips, forming the words, "I hope all you stupid fuckin' lip-readers are watching. Why don't you just blow me, you goofy deaf bastards." The TV station will enjoy taking the many phone calls.

I feel sorry for bisexuals. Can you imagine wanting to fuck everybody you meet? Jesus, think of all the phone numbers you'd come home with. Might as well walk around with the white pages under your arm.

Hitler never bothered with restaurant reservations; he just dropped by. And somehow they always found him a table.

I'm glad the *Peanuts* comic strip is finished; I never understood its appeal. I'm looking forward now to the disappearance of *Garfield* and *Doonesbury*.

One of the more pretentious political self-descriptions is "Libertarian." People think it puts them above the fray. It sounds fashionable and, to the uninitiated, faintly dangerous. Actually, it's just one more bullshit political philosophy.

When a plane crashes, and a lot of people die, I always wonder what happens to their frequent flier miles.

Why don't they have waiters in waiting rooms?

I'm glad Americans have trashed their national parks. I especially like that they can't blame it on Jews, blacks or immigrants. It was all done by ignorant, white-slob American tourists.

When you read about all the presidents who had affairs, you feel sorry for Gerald Ford. Apparently no one wanted to fuck him. Except Betty. And she was drunk a lot.

THE FOLLOWING STATEMENT IS TRUE.
THE ABOVE STATEMENT IS FALSE.

Many people think they have to lie to get out of jury duty. You don't have to lie; tell the judge the truth. Tell him you'll make a really good juror because you can spot guilty people just by looking at them. Explain that it has to do with how far apart their eyes are. I guarantee you'll be out of that courtroom before you can say "justice sucks."

You know what I like? A big fire in an apartment house.

Ecology note: In an economy measure, the number of bees in a squadron has been reduced from 35 to 20.

I often wonder if movie directors have credits at the end of their dreams?

SPORTS SHOULD BE FIXED: OVERTIME

Auto Racing

I'd like to improve auto racing. This is a sport that's very big in the South; a perfect marriage of fast cars and slow minds. I think if they want to liven up these races, what they ought to do is have one guy driving in the wrong direction. Simple thing: one guy, moving against the traffic. Maybe with a deer strapped to the hood, and a muffler dragging, makin' sparks. You could also stick three children with rickets in the backseat. Racing fans would appreciate seein' something familiar. Make 'em feel right at home.

Here's another thing that would increase the danger and excitement in these races: You offer an irresistibly huge sum of money—$50 million—to any driver who completes ten laps while driving in reverse. Doesn't matter which direction he's going, with or against the traffic; it's his choice. Fifty million dollars! Some guy would try it. Count on it. In fact, for $50 million you might wind up with everybody in the race goin' backward. Perfect metaphor for the South.

It would also be highly entertaining if the pit crews had to change tires right out on the track, during the race. I'd like to see them try those ten-second pit stops under some *really* stressful conditions. And maybe if you gave 'em longer hoses they could refuel the cars out there, too. Adds a fire hazard, heightens the danger, increases the fun. Just a thought.

And speakin' of danger, isn't it about time they eliminated that boring pace-car shit? They oughta start these races by havin' a couple of Air Force F-18's zippin' around the track, real low. Keep them ten

feet off the ground, so the locals can get a real good look. Just watchin'
them make those turns would be worth the whole trip to the track.
Most of those racing fans are soldier-sniffers and patriotic halfwits anyway, so I'm sure they'd be honored to have the occasional military jet
slam into the crowd and send a couple of hundred of them off to be
with Jesus.

And, speaking of such possibilities, it goes without saying that the
most satisfying part of auto racing is the high number of fatal accidents.
So maybe we could do a few things that would increase the frequency
of these accidents or, if not, at least make them a little more dangerous.

One idea I had, although it's decidedly offbeat, would be to spray
olive oil on the track about every twenty minutes. Not only would this
add driving excitement, it would produce an interesting aroma as it
mingled with the gasoline fumes, the stale beer, and the pervasive body
odor.

Another good accident enhancer would be requiring the drivers
to race single file, except for two short, 100-yard passing lanes at each
end of the track. Let them jockey for position just as they're heading
into the turns. And guess what? This might be the perfect spot for the
olive-oil release.

Here's another thrill provider: line the interiors of the cars with
plastic explosives rigged to go off when anything touches the exterior
of the car. Anything: the wall, another car, debris from the track. Shit,
you could probably make it sensitive enough so that one of those heavy
clouds of corn-dog farts that come rolling out of the grandstand from
time to time would set it off. And just think, the fart cloud itself would
probably add several lovely colors to the pyrotechnic display of the
explosion.

SEVEN DEATH WISHES

#1 You're in a leather bar with 200 heavily armed, wildly drunk, ex-convict, sadomasochistic butch lesbians. You climb on the bar and say, "Which one of you sweet little cupcakes wants the privilege of being the first in line to suck me off? If you're the lucky one, and you give me a real good blow job, I might do you a favor and throw you a quick fuck and let you cook me a nice meal. C'mon, line up, you repulsive cunts, and I'll change your sexual orientations. I dare you to cut off my balls!"

#2 Walking through the woods one day, you encounter a group of devil worshipers who are disemboweling a small boy. You tell them what they're doing is cowardly, unnatural, and morally wrong, and you're sure they would never try it on a grown-up. Especially one like yourself, who loves Jesus, and always wears his crucifix proudly. You also say that you just arrived from Australia, have no local friends or living relatives, and are planning to establish a Christian church called Fuck Lucifer. Then you order them to stay where they are, because you're leaving to get the police.

#3 You and your wife are the only nonbikers at a Hell's Angels' wedding, where all the others have been drinking, shooting methamphetamine, and smoking PCP for eleven straight days. At the height of the celebration, you whip out your dick, grab the bride's crotch, and shout to the crowd, "I understand you filthy, greasy asshole motorcycle cowards are supposed to be real good at gang rape, but I'll bet you can't fuck like me! Watch this!" You begin ripping the wedding gown off the bride, pointing out that your own wife is a virgin, and that you, yourself, have never been fucked in the ass.

#4 At a white supremacists' convention in remote Idaho, you take the stage wearing an ATF helmet and a Malcolm X T-shirt, and holding a United Nations flag. You perform a rap song that says morally and intellectually inferior white people should submit themselves to black rule and turn over their wives and daughters to black men as a way of apologizing for slavery. You mention that following your recent conversion to Judaism, you have become ashamed of your white skin and would gladly have it removed if you could just find a way to do it.

#5 Three sadistic sex maniacs have entered your house, and they find you naked in the shower. The most coherent among them asks if he can play with your genitals. You lose your temper and say, "Listen, you perverted, lunatic fuck, leave my sex organs alone. And tell your drooling, fruitcake buddies I would rather place my cock in that paper shredder located by the window, or stuff my testicles into the Cuisinart, which is in the kitchen on the right-hand shelf, than let you disgusting degenerates touch my private parts."

#6 While attending the First Communion of a Mafia boss's grandson, you suddenly begin to pistol-whip the boy's mother, screaming, "I'm gonna hit you some more, you ugly dago bitch, and if one of these greasy, dickless criminal morons who call themselves men makes a move on me, I'll break his guinea neck. I'm hungry! Make me some fuckin' spaghetti and go easy on the oil, ya hairy greaseball cunt!"

#7 You're standing in a crowded Harlem bar dressed in the robes of a Ku Klux Klan Grand Dragon, holding a Confederate flag, and singing "Dixie" in a real loud voice with a Mississippi accent. You jump on the bar, shit in the drink of a huge man with numerous razor scars on his face, wipe your ass with a picture of Martin Luther King, and yell at the man, "Hey, boy! Get your momma down here, I want some dark meat. And get that fuckin' jungle-bunny music off the juke box, or I'm gonna start killin' me some boogies!"

Have a nice afterlife.

MONOPOLY

I never did well at Monopoly. I guess I don't have a business mind. Oh, I'd usually manage to own a couple of railroads. And Water Works, of course. I'm not a complete asshole; I know a monopoly when I see one. Everybody needs water. But it always frustrated me that the other guys wouldn't let me build houses on Water Works. They said it was zoning or some shit like that. I think they were jealous that I had vision. The worst fight I ever got into was when I tried to put hotels on the Electric Company. Vision.

As far as other properties were concerned, naturally I'd snap up Baltic Avenue as soon as that became available.

"How much is that son of a bitch? Sixty bucks? Gimme that mother. I gotta have a place to live."

About the best thing I'd ever own would be one or two properties in the light blue series. Maybe Oriental Avenue. No houses, of course. Just an excavation or two. That's about all I ever had on my property—plans. Surveyor's marks. I just couldn't get financing. All my friends would have shopping centers, malls, condominiums, industrial parks. And they liked to rub it in.

"Oh boy, Carlin, you're comin' down my side of the board now! Get ready to pay up!"

"Ohh, no! Please God, gimme a big one."

Then I'd roll.

"Hot shit!! A twelve! Thank you, God! JUMP! JUMP! JUMP! JUMP! JUMP! JUMP! JUMP! JUMP! JUMP! JUMP! JUMP! JUMP! Fuck you, Tony. I ain't even stoppin' on your side. Fuck you and Boardwalk, too!"

"That's all right, Carlin, you'll be around again."

Of course, you can't move your token until you remember which one is yours.

"Which one is mine? Am I the hat? I could swear I was the hat. No, that was yesterday. Wait! I know. The racing car. I'm the racing car. Hey, who's the ship? Richie, are you the ship?"

"No, he's not the ship, I'm the ship. I get the ship every game. Don't even touch the ship." Tony was the biggest guy.

None of them wanted to be the iron. Too feminine.

The worst token to have was the cannon. The big gun. It was the only topheavy token. It kept falling over. Throw the dice anywhere near it, and it fell on its side. And then some anal retentive would say, "Who has the gun? Are you the gun? Would ya pick it up, please? And you, Paulie, are you *in* jail or just visiting? Well, if you're just visiting, put the car on the *side* of the jail, not on the actual jail part."

Some guys really cared. That's why they won.

I never won, but I was always in there at the end. Because I had all the one-dollar bills. Twenty-five hundred dollars in singles, and they needed me to make change.

I would try to borrow money.

"Please, Tony. Just five bucks. I wanna buy some gum."

"Fuck you, Carlin. I'll give you five bucks for Water Works."

"Ten."

"Seven-fifty."

"Tony, they don't have a fifty-cent bill."

"Tough shit. Tear a dollar in half."

No, I wasn't very good at the game, but I spent a lot of time landing on Chance. And I always tried to buy it. I got in more fights trying to buy Chance.

I'd move my token. "... three, four, five, six, seven, eight, nine ... Chance!" Turn over the card, a little man with a hat: "Two hundred dollars for being an asshole."

"Hey, Richie, shuffle those cards, will ya? That's the second time I got that one."